Solar Cooking for Home and Camp

0 11557 03402 8

Solar Cooking for Home and Camp

LINDA FREDERICK YAFFE

STACKPOLE
BOOKS

Published by
STACKPOLE BOOKS
5067 Ritter Road
Mechanicsburg, PA 17055
www.stackpolebooks.com

Printed in the United States

First edition

10 9 8 7 6 5 4 3 2 1

Cover photograph by Solar Cookers International
Cover design by Caroline Stover
Illustrations by the author

Library of Congress Cataloging-in-Publication Data
Yaffe, Linda Frederick.
  Solar cooking for home and camp / Linda Frederick Yaffe.
     p. cm.
  Includes index.
  ISBN-13: 978-0-8117-3402-8 (alk. paper)
  ISBN-10: 0-8117-3402-1 (alk. paper)
  1. Solar cookery. I. Title.

TX835.5.Y34 2007
641.5'8—dc22
                                        2007003173

In fond memory of my beloved parents-in-law:
Charles D. Yaffe (1910–2006)
and Frayda Goodstein Yaffe (1912–2006)

The sun himself shines heartily, and shares the joy he brings.
— Ralph Waldo Emerson, "The World-Soul," 1899

It is so much pleasanter and wholesomer to be warmed by the sun when you can, than by a fire.
—Journal of Henry D. Thoreau, November 8, 1850

CONTENTS

CHAPTER ONE

MAKING AND USING YOUR OWN SOLAR COOKER

Solar cooking is free, clean, simple, and fun. It will save you time and money and also save the earth's finite resources. More than just a novelty, solar cooking is a healthy way of life. It's the most fun you'll ever have while doing the right thing.

Imagine sitting in a car with the windows closed on a bright, sunny day. You notice that the temperature inside the car is much hotter than the temperature outside. This is the greenhouse effect: Sunlight shines through the windows and is converted to heat. The heat is soaked up and retained by the objects inside, such as the upholstered seats, especially if they are dark colored. This built-up heat is then trapped inside the car. Solar cookers employ the same principle to quietly, gently cook your food. The process is basic: Put raw ingredients in a covered pot, place the pot in the solar cooker, and point the cooker toward the sun.

Solar cookers are major home appliances, but they are simple, lightweight, and low-tech. And unlike other major appliances, you can build one yourself in a few hours, and it costs nothing to operate. *Solar Cooking for Home and Camp* shows you how to make these wonderful appliances from common, readily available materials. Instructions are provided for building two types of solar cookers: a box cooker and a portable, folding panel cooker. Or, if you prefer, you can buy a prebuilt solar cooker (see Resources). The book also includes 165 easy recipes designed especially for solar cooking. Many of the dishes can be assembled quickly in the morning and placed in a covered pot in the solar cooker. Then you just set the cooker in any sunny location—a south-facing porch or balcony, on the roof of your house, in your back garden, or on a picnic table at your campsite—and aim it toward the midday or afternoon sun. While you go off to work or play, the solar cooker does its magic, and you'll come home to a hot meal at dinnertime—all without smoke or fumes, an overheated kitchen, pots to stir, or the use of fossil fuels. Plus, there are no concerns about overcooking; although a large casserole will be fully cooked in one to two hours, the dish can be held in the solar cooker all day.

Your solar cooker will become your favorite way to prepare meals because it is convenient and labor-saving. Vegetables don't need to be parboiled before being stuffed and baked. Pasta used in combination baked dishes doesn't have to be boiled and drained first. Foods such as meats and vegetables don't need to be marinated; the solar cooker marinates and cooks, all in one step. Delicious fresh fruit jam can be made without stirring or messy boilovers. Frozen dishes placed in the solar cooker defrost, cook, and then keep warm for hours, allowing you to dine whenever you're ready. Cleanup afterward is easier, too. With no burned-on food residue, pots quickly wipe clean.

With naturally gentle, slow solar cooking—and little or no water added—your meals will be moist, flavorful, and full of nutrients. So reserve your conventional oven or camp stove for nighttime or days of inclement weather. On sunny or mostly sunny days with at least four hours of direct sunlight, you can cook with solar power.

Solar Box Cooker

The solar box cooker is made from two cardboard boxes lined with aluminum foil, the smaller nested inside the larger. A cardboard lid with a window made from a nylon oven cooking bag and topped by a foil-covered cardboard reflector completes this easy project. The cardboard solar box cooker was devised in the 1970s by solar innovator and activist Barbara Kerr, in collaboration with Sherry Cole. Their simple, lightweight design has made solar box cookers easy and inexpensive to construct and use. Box cookers are dependable over a long cooking season each year. Since they utilize both reflected and retained heat, box cookers hold the heat well on partly cloudy days. They excel at long, slow cooking—perfect for simmered foods such as beans and stews—and they are excellent for baking. Although this simple box takes just a few hours to make, it will provide you with great meals for many years to come. Assemble the following tools and materials, and you'll be ready to go.

Materials

Three or four large cardboard boxes: one for the inner box, one for
the outer box, plus additional cardboard to make a lid, a reflector, and four interior insulating panels

One roll of masking tape

One 75-foot roll of regular-weight (not heavyweight) aluminum
foil

Eight ounces of nontoxic glue, such as Elmer's glue, or flour paste
(see recipe on page 5)

Two or three empty toilet paper rolls

Several pounds of insulation: wool fabric scraps, crumpled newspaper, or shredded office paper

One nylon oven cooking bag, large or turkey size

One wire coat hanger

One jar or spray can of black, nontoxic tempera (water-based)
paint

Cardboard Boxes

When choosing your cardboard boxes, keep in mind that a large, shallow solar cooker works best. A cooker that is too deep is hard to heat,
largely because the tall sides of the box create more shadows, but also

because it loses more heat from the sides. Look for recycled corrugated cardboard boxes that originally held large electrical appliances. They are sturdy and have large surfaces, and the thick-walled, double-honeycomb layer of corrugation makes a long-lived cooker.

First, find an inner box that is just tall enough to accommodate your solar cooking pots and long and wide enough to hold a baking sheet (it's a good idea to measure and record the dimensions of your cookware before you begin the search for a suitable box). Choose an inner box that is one inch taller than your largest lidded pot and one inch longer and wider than your baking sheet. Dark baking sheets make good trays inside a box cooker; the dark metal absorbs and holds heat, and the tray protects the bottom of the cooker. Plan to leave a baking sheet inside the cooker permanently. In general, you'll want a box that is at least large enough for a ten-by-fifteen-inch lidded turkey roaster or roomy enough for two or three smaller round pots, such as eight- or nine-inch-diameter black enamelware pots (tips on choosing the best pots for solar cooking are provided later in this chapter).

Then look for an outer box that is about an inch or two larger on all sides than the inner box. Don't make the cooker so large that you can't move it easily. Cardboard box cookers are lightweight, but they can be bulky. Choose an outer box that you can get your arms around.

Oven Bag

A nylon oven cooking bag—lighter weight and easier to handle than glass—will form the window of your solar cooker. Oven Bags, made by Reynolds, are designed to withstand heat up to 400 degrees. Don't use ordinary plastic bags; they'll melt. A "turkey size" Reynolds Oven Bag is 19 by 23½ inches—large enough to provide a big window for most large cookers. If you need an even larger window, two Oven Bags can be cut open and the edges glued together. For smaller cookers, use "large size" Oven Bags, which measure 16 by 17½ inches.

Glue

You'll need glue to bond the aluminum foil to the cardboard. If you'd like to make your own, stir up some homemade flour paste using this recipe:

Flour Paste

This recipe makes 2 cups of paste—more than enough for the construction of a large solar cooker. Flour paste is ready to use immediately (as soon as it's cool enough to handle).

1. Place in a small bowl:
     ⅓ cup white flour
2. Slowly stir in:
     ⅔ cup cold water
3. Bring to a boil in a saucepan:
     1½ cups water
4. Pour the flour and water mixture into the saucepan while stirring continuously; then reduce heat and simmer, stirring occasionally, for 5 minutes, or until thick.
5. Cool. Store excess paste in a covered jar in the refrigerator for up to 2 weeks. Thin with warm water to reuse.

Tools

  Utility knife or other sturdy, sharp knife
  Straightedge
  Soft, dark pencil
  Brush to spread glue or paste
  Wire cutters

Assembly Instructions

1. Trim the height of the smaller (inner) box, if necessary. Mark the corners of the smaller box with a pencil one inch above the height of your tallest pot. Slit the corners of the box down to the pencil marks; then use a straight-edge and pencil to draw lines on the *inside* of the box connecting the marks at the corners. Lightly score the cardboard with a knife

along the pencil lines on the *inside* of the box. Then fold the sides of the box down and *outward* along the scores.

2. Stand both boxes side by side. If the larger box is more than an inch and a half taller than the scored height of the smaller one, mark the corners of the larger box 1½ inches above the smaller box. Use a yardstick and pencil to draw lines on the *outside* of the box, connecting the pencil marks at the corners. Slit the corners of

the larger box down to the marks, lightly score the cardboard with a knife along the pencil lines on the *outside* of the box, and fold the sides *inward* along the scores. Trim the excess cardboard from the ends of all four flaps of the larger box so that they just meet in the center, creating a shorter covered box.

3. Close both boxes. Use a few pieces of masking tape to temporarily hold the lid of the larger box neatly closed. Center the smaller box on top of the larger box and trace around it, marking the top of the larger box. Remove the smaller box and set it aside. Using a utility knife, cut around the traced line on the larger box, removing the

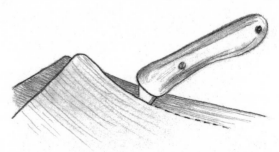

center of the top of the box and the masking tape. This hole will accommodate the smaller box.

4. Glue regular-weight aluminum foil onto the entire inside of the larger box. (Regular-weight foil is more flexible than heavyweight foil and adheres more smoothly to the cardboard, creating a shiny, reflective surface.) Use a brush to coat nontoxic glue or flour paste over the interior bottom and sides (thin the glue or paste with water to spreading consistency, if necessary). The foil doesn't need to be even; overlaps are fine. Simply cover the interior as completely as possible, and glue the edges down securely. Once the in-

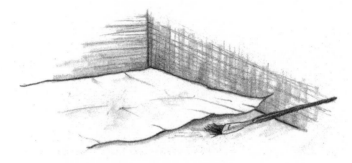

terior is covered with foil, glue the remaining parts of the top flaps together, and glue foil onto the tops of the flaps.

5. Glue aluminum foil onto the inside of the smaller box, completely covering the bottom and sides. Glue foil onto the insides of the flaps, extending the foil three to four inches beyond the top of the box.

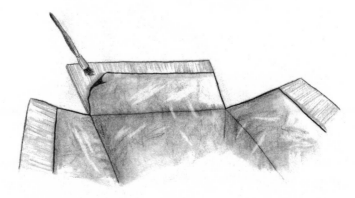

6. Cut four cardboard panels one-quarter inch smaller in both length and width than the interior sides of the larger box. Glue foil to one side of each panel. Insert the panels loosely against the inside walls of the larger box, foil sides toward the center of the box. These panels will provide extra insulation.

7. Cut two or three empty toilet paper rolls into six pieces that are each 1½ inches long. Stand these six pieces in the bottom of the larger box, to serve as pillars to support the smaller box. Spread nontoxic insulation around the bottom of the box. Since synthetics tend to produce gases when the cooker heats up, choose natural

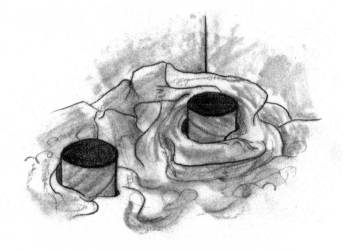

materials for insulation. Use any combination of the following: clean fabric scraps or old blankets, sweaters, or other garments, preferably woolen; loosely crumpled sheets of newspaper; or crumpled or shredded paper. Loosely slip more insulation in the space between the foiled panels and the outer walls of the box. Don't pack the insulation too tightly; you want air spaces between the pieces of insulation to trap the heat.

8. Insert the smaller box inside the larger box. Use the utility knife to trim the flaps of the smaller box flush with the edges of the larger box. Then glue the flaps of the smaller box to the top of the larger box. After applying glue, hold the flaps in place temporarily with masking tape; remove the tape when the glue is dry. The base of the solar box cooker is now complete.

9. To make the lid, set the cooker base on a piece of corrugated cardboard that is at least six inches longer and six inches wider than the base. Trace the outline of the base onto the cardboard. Then mark the cardboard three inches beyond the base on all sides. Connect the marks, using a yardstick, to form the outline of the lid's lip. Cut around the outline.

10. Score the lid lightly with a knife along the pencil lines, and continue scoring straight out to the edges of the lid. Place the lid on the box. Check for fit; then fold the lips of the sides down over the

box. Make four slits, one at each corner of the lid, so that the corners of the lid overlap.

11. To measure and cut a window hole, remove the lid from the box. Lay it out flat, wrong side up. The window needs to lie as closely as possible over the walls of the cooker base. Measure the thickness of the cooker base's walls—front, back, and sides. Mark the lid to match these measurements. Draw four lines with a yardstick. Cut along these lines; then remove and discard the center of the lid.

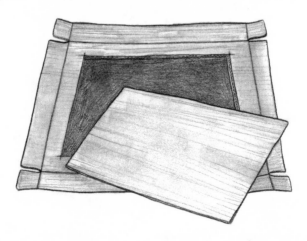

12. Still working with the lid upside down, choose an appropriate-sized Reynolds Oven Bag for a window. When closed and flat, the bag needs to cover the window hole and extend at least one inch beyond the opening on all sides. If the bag is too long, trim the open

end to fit; securely glue the open edges of the trimmed Oven Bag together to prevent condensation accumulation inside the bag. Then glue the closed bag to the inside edges of the window hole.

13. Glue the corners of the lid. Hold the glued corners in place with masking tape. Remove the tape when the glue is dry.

14. To make the reflector, cut a piece of corrugated cardboard the same length as the top of the lid and the width of the lid plus 3½ inches. Lay the reflector cardboard on top of the cooker so the sides and front are even with the lid. Lightly score the reflector along the *inner* edge of the cooker's back wall and along the back of the *outside* of the cooker. Glue aluminum foil to the inside of the reflector. Keep the foil as smooth as possible, pushing air bubbles from the

center to the edges. Then glue the reflector to the top and back of the lid. Hold the reflector in place with masking tape; remove the tape when the glue is dry.

15. Make an adjustable prop holder for the reflector. Cut two strips of corrugated cardboard 1½ inches wide and 10 inches long with corrugations running *parallel* to the *width* of the strips. Glue one piece to the top righthand side of the lid and the other above it on the righthand foiled side of the reflector. Keep the prop holders in place with masking tape until the glue is dry; then remove the tape.

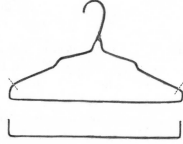

16. Make a prop. Use wire cutters to snip off the length of the bottom of an ordinary wire coat hanger plus one to two inches beyond. Bend the ends of the hanger into 90-degree angles. Insert the ends into the corrugations of the cardboard. The reflector can then be angled to direct the sunlight into the center of the cooker.

17. Insert a black tray into the bottom of the cooker to absorb heat, improving the cooker's efficiency, and to protect the bottom of the cooker from wear. Dark metal is the best choice for heat retention, such as a dark baking sheet. If you don't have a dark baking sheet

that fits your cooker, you can make your own tray. Cut a piece of cardboard or metal flashing to fit the bottom of the cooker's interior. Glue foil to one side of the cardboard and paint the foil with nontoxic flat black paint, or paint one side of the flashing black. Set the tray in the cooker, black side up.

18. Your solar box cooker is now complete. Set the cooker propped open in full sunlight for a few hours to fully dry the glue and paint.

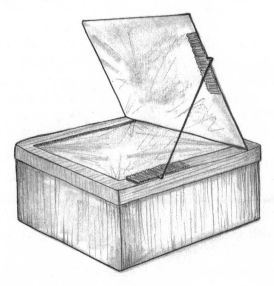

This simple cardboard solar box cooker will last—if protected from in-clement weather—for ten years or longer. The foil can be patched if it becomes worn, and the Oven Bag window can easily be replaced. When the solar cooker finally wears out, the appliance is easily disas-sembled, and all parts can be recycled.

Folding Panel Cooker

This portable, folding panel cooker can be made in a couple of hours. It uses reflective heat from foil-covered cardboard panels directed toward a pot or pots encased in nylon oven cooking bags to retain heat. The panel cooker's central flat surface can hold one large or two small cook-ing pots. The panel cooker was developed by Roger Bernard of France and Barbara Kerr of the United States, with additional work by Edwin Pejack, Jay Campbell, and Bev Blum of Solar Cookers International. This type of cooker has done much to improve daily life in fuel-poor, sun-rich countries by allowing people to cook food and pasteurize water safely and easily. With no box to preheat, these cookers are "on" as soon as the sun hits them. The panel cooker is an excellent children's project, providing a vivid demonstration of solar power.

Materials

> One three-by-four-foot piece of corrugated cardboard (use an
> opened recycled carton, or buy a sheet of cardboard)
> One small roll of regular-weight (not heavyweight) aluminum foil
> Eight ounces of nontoxic glue, such as Elmer's glue, or flour paste
> (see recipe on page 5)
> Clothespins, large paper clips, or binder clips
> One or two nylon oven cooking bags, turkey or large size

Tools

> Utility knife or other sturdy, sharp knife
> Spoon or other blunt utensil
> Yardstick
> Soft, dark pencil
> Brush to spread glue or paste

Assembly Instructions

1. If your corrugated cardboard is larger than three by four feet, trim it to that size. If you are using an opened recycled cardboard box, tape the slits closed to form a solid piece.
2. Use these measurements to pencil the cooker shape onto the cardboard.
3. Cut out the shape of the cooker along the penciled outline.
4. On the *inside* of the cooker, pencil in dotted fold lines (as shown on the next page), and cut two 4½-inch-long slots at a 60-degree angle. Use a spoon handle or butter knife to lightly score the penciled fold lines on the *inside* of the cooker. Then use a table edge or a yardstick to evenly bend the cardboard inward along the fold lines.
5. With the cooker inside up, use a brush to apply nontoxic glue or paste to the cardboard. Glue regular-weight aluminum foil, shiny

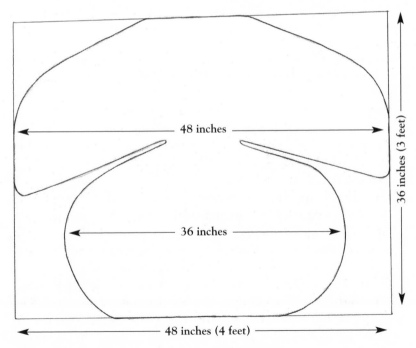

Step 2: Pencil the cooker shape onto the cardboard.

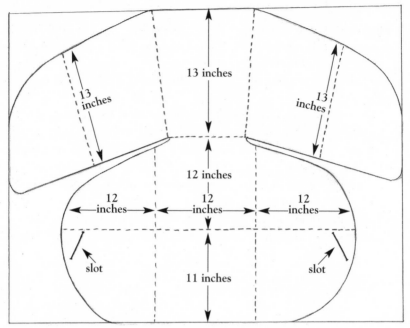

13 inches

13 inches

13 inches

13 inches

12 inches

12 inches

12 inches

12 inches

11 inches

slot

slot

Step 4: Pencil the fold lines and slots onto the cardboard.

side up, over the entire inside of the cooker. Seams and overlaps are fine; just keep the foil as smooth as possible, pushing air bubbles from the center to the edges. Cut two slots through the foil that match the slots through the cardboard.

6. Set the cooker flat, and let it dry.

7. To assemble the panel cooker, lay the cooker foil side (inside) up. Bend up along the front (shorter side) fold line, and bend the back (taller side) up and around along the fold line. Slide the corners of the back into the slots. Clamp the inserted corners on the outside of the cooker with clothespins, large paper clips, or binder clips.

8. To use the cooker, place food inside a thin, dark metal pot with a tight-fitting lid. Place the pot inside a nylon Reynolds Oven Bag. Twist the bag closed, leaving a thin layer of air around the pot inside the bag, and fasten tightly with a twist tie. Place the pot on the flat surface in the center of the cooker.

9. Face the cooker toward the sun. If you are leaving it to cook all day, aim it with the front (shorter side) toward the midday or afternoon sun. Adjust the front of the cooker to reflect, not block, the sun.

Tips for Successful Solar Cooking

Cookware

Although any ovenproof pots and pans can be used in a solar cooker, for best results, use covered metal pots that are wide, shallow, light-weight, and dark—preferably black, because black absorbs heat. Solar Cookers International offers dark enamelware cooking pots by mail (see Resources). Blackened camping pots also work well.

Shiny pots reflect heat away from the pot instead of absorbing it. To increase the efficiency of shiny or light-colored cookware, coat the outsides of the pots and lids with nontoxic flat black paint. Alternatively, cover shiny pots and lids with dark cloths. Avoid using aluminum foil as a pot lid in a solar cooker, because foil also reflects heat. Ensure that the lids are tight-fitting. The covered pots work like little "ovens" inside the cooker: the lid both holds in the heat and keeps condensation inside the cooker to a minimum.

Although thin-walled metal cookware heats much more quickly, heavy cookware—such as black cast-iron or dark-colored, thick-walled pottery—holds the heat for a longer time, once it is heated through.

Location, Timing, and Weather

Solar cookers can be used in most inhabited areas of the world— anywhere between 60 degrees north and 60 degrees south of the equator. A useful rule of thumb is that you can use a solar cooker on any sunny day and during any season when the length of your shadow on the ground is shorter than your height—typically, four to eight months of the year.

Choose a south- or southwest-facing spot for your solar cooker. On a cold day, winds can cool the cooker, so a buffer such as a wall or a fence can significantly raise the cooker's temperature. Solar cookers can be set on a platform or a table, on a rooftop, or on the ground. They can be placed in a garden cart, wagon, wheelbarrow, or serving cart for easy maneuverability.

In terms of timing, the solar cooker is forgiving. In the recipes in this book, all cooking times are approximate. Most dishes can be held for several extra hours in the cooker. So get the food into the solar cooker early in the day, and don't worry about it; serve dinner whenever you're ready. Solar cooking is remarkably stress-free.

Choose foods and recipes that match the weather. On clear, sunny days, you can cook beans or whole potatoes all day long or bake a heat-loving bread or cake at midday after preheating the cooker for a couple of hours. Even days with overcast skies can be solar cooking days; the food will simply cook more slowly. On low-sun days, choose recipes containing food that is cut into small pieces for quicker cooking. For example, a partly cloudy day may not provide enough heat to fully bake a whole raw potato, but the same potato grated or diced in a dish with other ingredients will cook easily. Or try boiling food briefly or giving it a head start in a conventional oven before finishing the cooking in the solar cooker. Likewise, use hot rather than cold water in the dishes you're assembling.

If a sunny morning turns into a cloudy afternoon, cover box cookers with warm blankets and use the retained heat to complete cooking. Alternatively, in case of rain, bring the box cooker indoors and cover it with blankets. Be flexible; if you lose the sun, you can always finish cooking in a conventional oven or on a camp stove.

Useful Accessories

A food processor greatly speeds the preparation of most recipes in this book. You can quickly combine the ingredients in the morning and enjoy a ready-to-eat hot meal when you get home.

Experiment using an accurate oven thermometer and an instant-read probe thermometer (see Resources) to learn what your cooker can do in different conditions.

Raise your cooker's temperature by placing a firebrick or a small, flat rock inside underneath the pots. Preheat the brick or rock inside the Oven Bag of a panel cooker, and then set your pot inside the bag on top of the heated rock. Alternatively, set three or four small stones under the pot inside the Oven Bag to increase warm airflow. Tightly covered, dark-colored glass bottles partially filled with water (don't overfill—the water will expand) increase heat as well; set them next to the cooking pots. Once they are heated, water bottles, rocks, or firebricks help hold in the heat late in the day.

Use wire baking racks to increase heat flow underneath the pots inside a box cooker. Set the rack on top of the cooker's tray. Use a tall rack from a steamer pot to raise a flat dish much higher, giving foods even more heat circulation and bringing them into fuller sunlight inside the cooker.

Food Preparation and Placement

Solar cookers are healthy cookers. You can use less water—or none at all—to cook many foods. The solar cooker retains ingredients' moisture and nutrients as they cook. As a result, soups and stews need less liquid, and most vegetables require no additional water to cook. If too much moisture accumulates in the cooker, vent it by opening the panel cooker's Oven Bag or propping open the box cooker's lid slightly.

Cut food into uniform pieces for even cooking, and don't overcrowd the cooker. The more food it contains, the more heat required to cook it. Try to allow an inch or two between the cooker's sides and the pots and between the pots themselves. A thin layer of food in a wide, shallow pot cooks more rapidly than food piled deeply in a tall, narrow pot. To create a dish for four to six people, either use one large pot, such as a ten-by-fifteen-inch covered roasting pan, or divide the food between two small pots for best results.

Food placed near the top of the pot, where the heat is concentrated, becomes hotter than food at the bottom. A preheated firebrick or rock underneath the pot will increase the bottom heat.

Food that has been refrigerated overnight or has been frozen can be placed in the solar cooker early. The food will warm and defrost, then cook, and then stay warm for dinner.

Summary

Your solar cooker will cook food more quickly when:

There is full sun.

The sun is high in the sky (midday year round, or during the summer months).

The cooker is located in a south-facing area and protected from cold winds.

There is only a small amount of liquid, or no extra liquid, in the pot.

The ingredients are cut into small pieces.

The pots are dark colored, preferably black, for better heat absorption.

The pots are made of thin metal that heats quickly.

The pots are short and wide.

The solar box cooker is large and shallow.

The cooker is not overcrowded.

Your solar cooker will cook food more slowly when:

The day is partly cloudy.

The sun is low in the sky (early or late in the day year-round, or during the winter months).

The cooker is exposed to cold winds.

There is a lot of liquid in the pot, such as a large quantity of soup.

The ingredients are in large pieces.

The pots are light colored and shiny, reflecting heat away from the food.

The pots are made of a thick material that takes a long time to heat.

The pots are tall and narrow.
The solar box cooker is narrow and deep.
The cooker is crowded with large quantities of food.

Most of the foods you enjoy every day can be successfully cooked by the sun. Enjoy the recipes in this book; then experiment with your own favorite foods and recipes to learn how much your solar cooker can do for you.

Camping Solar

Astronomer and physicist Samuel P. Langley—a lifelong solar innovator—used a solar cooker in 1881 to prepare meals while leading a scientific climbing party on Mount Whitney. This was the first recorded use of solar cooking in the United States. With a solar cooker, you too can enjoy freshly baked breads and cakes, pasteurized drinking water, plenty of hot water for washing up, and delicious cooked meals in camp—all without using a campfire.

The recipes in this book can travel, with just a little preparation before you leave. Those recommended for camping are marked with the camp symbol. Mix dry ingredients for baked goods at home; then simply add liquids in camp. For even greater convenience, use commercially dried milk and eggs (see Resources) rather than fresh. Be sure to label and date every bag of premixed ingredients so you know exactly what's in the bag and how much water to add in camp. Casseroles, stews, or soups can also be made well ahead of time and frozen. When you pack your ice chest, set the frozen dish near the top. The descending cold will help keep the rest of the food fresh. Once you get to the park or campground, simply slide the defrosted casserole into the solar cooker; then add water to your premixed dry ingredients, shape it into a loaf, and place it next to the casserole. Later on, you'll enjoy a steaming hot homemade meal and fresh bread, all without the smoke, pollution, safety concerns, and constant tending that are an inevitable part of campfire cooking.

Camp symbol

You can use your solar cooker in camp throughout the day, but don't leave food unattended in bear country. Pasteurize water anytime during the morning or afternoon (see details later in this chapter). Solar pasteurization is far more convenient than filtering, boiling, or chemically treating your drinking water. While you are heating up your midday meal, you can also bake bread or a cake. Then, when lunch is ready, put a frozen or refrigerated casserole into the cooker for dinner.

Either design of solar cooker described in this book can make car camping more fun. The box-style cooker, though bulkier, fits inside the trunk of a small car and works well for car camping. The folding panel cooker, which is extremely light and takes up very little space in your vehicle, is also perfect for car camping. It can even be folded up, strapped to a backpack, and carried to a secluded base camp.

Supplemented with a small camp stove or a tiny wood cooking fire for early-morning use or on cloudy or rainy days, solar cookers are perfect for trouble-free camping. They are so safe that they can even be used in areas that prohibit campfires and gas stoves.

Safety and Emergencies

Physical Safety

Solar cookers are bright. Wear sunglasses whenever you're putting food into or removing it from your solar cooker. Stand in front of the cooker with your back to the sun.

A folding panel solar cooker can easily be stored in your car, house, or garage, making it a fine backup appliance to provide you with hot food and treated drinking water during power outages and other emergencies. Determine beforehand where you can access untreated water, and then use your solar cooker to pasteurize it. Also keep on hand a supply of ready-to-heat canned or dried (not frozen) food and treated water for immediate use. It's a good idea to have backup cooking equipment, such as a camp stove and fuel or a wood-burning stove and dry, burnable materials, for cooking on cloudy, rainy, or snowy days or for nighttime cooking.

Water and Milk Pasteurization

Use your solar cooker to eliminate the bacteria, viruses, and other microbes from human feces that may be present in untreated water. To pasteurize water, bring it to 150 degrees in a covered pot inside your solar cooker; bring milk to 160 degrees by the same method. This takes about sixty to ninety minutes per liter. Use an instant-read probe thermometer to check the temperature. Solar Cookers International (see Resources) offers water pasteurization indicators that can be placed inside a pot of water or milk; they show at a glance when the liquid has been safely pasteurized.

Food Safety

Use an accurate thermometer to ensure that food is cooked thoroughly and thus help you avoid food-borne illnesses. To test pieces of meat, fish, or poultry for doneness, use an accurate probe thermometer placed in the center of the meat (avoid touching the bone) to determine whether it has reached a safe temperature throughout. Beef, veal, and lamb must reach a minimum internal temperature of 145 degrees; pork and ground beef must reach 160 degrees; and poultry should be cooked to 165 degrees.

According to the United States Department of Agriculture's food safety guidelines, pathogens can grow and multiply at temperatures between 40 and 140 degrees—known as the "danger zone." It is essential to keep perishable hot foods hot and cold foods cold. Perishable foods include protein-containing foods such as meat, cooked dried beans, milk, and eggs. These foods should not remain in the danger zone for more than a couple of hours. An accurate thermometer can show you at a glance if your food is cooling too rapidly after it has been cooked.

If the weather is changing and you are losing sun, it may be best to complete the cooking using a conventional method. Alternatively, if the food in your solar cooker is cooling down, bring it to a boil or place it briefly in the kitchen oven to bring the temperature up to 140 degrees or higher; then replace it in the solar cooker and cover the cooker with blankets to retain the heat while the cooking is completed. If there are shadows on your solar box cooker, close the lid and throw a tarp, towels, sleeping bag, or blankets over it to retain the heat. To be safe, let your thermometer be your guide.

CHAPTER TWO

SIDE DISHES AND SNACKS

Appetizers

Bean Nachos

Serves 12

1. Spread evenly on a dark metal tray:
   1 pound whole-grain tortilla chips
2. Drop by tablespoons onto the chips:
   30 ounces refried beans
   1 cup salsa
3. Sprinkle over the top:
   12 ounces mild white cheese, such as Monterey Jack, shredded (makes about 3 cups)
4. Place the uncovered tray in the solar cooker for 1 hour, or until the beans are heated and the cheese is melted. Serve warm.

Hot Bean Dip

Serves 6

1. Combine in a pot:
   16 ounces refried beans
   8 ounces cream cheese, softened
   ¾ cup salsa or 8 ounces diced green chilies, mild, moderate, or hot
   1¼ cups shredded Monterey Jack or mozzarella cheese
   2 ounces ripe olives, drained and minced
2. Cover and place in the solar cooker for 2 hours.

3. Stir in any of the following before serving:
> **2 scallions, minced**
> **2 tablespoons minced fresh cilantro**
> **squeeze of fresh lemon juice**
4. Serve with tortilla chips or pita bread slices.

Quesadillas
Serves 8

1. Have ready:
> **8 corn tortillas, 8-inch diameter**
2. Place 4 of the tortillas in the bottom of a large oiled pot. Spread evenly over the tortillas:
> **½ cup salsa**
> **1½ cups any variety shredded cheese**
> **4 ounces fresh mushrooms, thinly sliced**
> **1 red or green bell pepper, diced**
3. Top with the remaining 4 tortillas.
4. Cover and place in the solar cooker for 2 hours.
5. Cut into wedges and serve warm or at room temperature.

Savory Cheddar Bread Pudding
Serves 10

Serve this as an appetizer, a side dish, or a light meal.
1. Spread in a large oiled pot:
> **5 cups bread (about 6 slices) cut into ½- to 1-inch cubes**
2. Sprinkle over the bread:
> **1¼ cups shredded sharp cheddar cheese**
3. Beat together in a large bowl:
> **2 eggs or ½ cup egg whites**
> **5 cups milk**
> **1 tablespoon sugar**
> **2 tablespoons prepared mustard**
> **1 tablespoon olive oil**
> **1 teaspoon salt**
> **½ teaspoon minced fresh rosemary, or ¼ teaspoon dried**

4. Pour the milk mixture over the bread cubes. Cover and place in the solar cooker for 3 hours.
5. Cut into small squares and serve warm.

Hot Crab Dip

Serves 6

1. Stir together in a large bowl:

> **8 ounces cream cheese, softened**
> **2 cups plain yogurt**
> **4 cloves garlic, minced**
> **½ teaspoon salt**
> **⅛ teaspoon hot sauce**
> **1 pound crabmeat, flaked**

2. Spread the mixture evenly in a large oiled pot. Sprinkle over the top:

> **½ cup grated Parmesan cheese**

3. Cover and place in the solar cooker for 1 hour.
4. Serve warm with tortilla chips, crackers, or raw vegetable sticks.

Sweet Potato Squares

Serves 12

1. Spread evenly in an oiled pot:

> **3 raw, dark orange sweet potatoes, scrubbed but not peeled, and shredded**
> **3 scallions, minced**
> **1 cup grated Parmesan cheese**

2. Beat together in a medium bowl:

> **4 eggs or 1 cup egg whites**
> **12 ounces evaporated milk**
> **1 tablespoon whole wheat flour**
> **½ teaspoon salt**
> **½ teaspoon freshly ground black pepper**
> **½ teaspoon ground nutmeg**

3. Pour the egg mixture over the potatoes and stir to coat. Cover and place in the solar cooker for 5 hours.
4. Cut into small squares and serve warm or at room temperature.

Snacks

Sun-Dried Fruits and Vegetables

It's easy and inexpensive to dry healthy seasonal treats using your solar cooker's radiant heat.

1. Wash (and peel, core, and seed, if necessary) and then thinly slice any fresh fruits or vegetables. Some fruits, such as seedless grapes and small berries, can be dried whole. The thicker the slices, the slower the drying.
2. Arrange the slices on dark metal trays; if the slices are fragile, such as ripe strawberries or peaches, lightly oil the trays first.
3. To use a solar panel cooker: Set the uncovered tray of fruit or vegetable slices in the panel cooker. Do not use an oven cooking bag. Adjust the front panel of the cooker to give the tray full sunlight. To use a solar box cooker: With the lid of the cooker closed and the reflector propped open, put a piece of cardboard over the window, and place the uncovered tray of fruits or vegetables on top of the cardboard. Angle the reflector to concentrate the sunlight on the center of the tray.
4. The concentrated heat from the reflector tends to keep bugs away, but if you see any bugs landing on the food, cover the tray with any fine-mesh nylon net fabric (see Resources).
5. Most fruits and vegetables dry in 3 to 12 hours. If the fruit isn't dry by the end of the day, bring the tray inside overnight and complete drying the next day.

Dried Apples   *2 cups (3 ounces of dried apples)*

When sliced and dried, 6 whole apples weigh only 3 ounces; they are perfect for backpack or lunch-box snacks.

1. Peel, core, and slice:
   6 large apples
2. Arrange the slices in a single layer on dark metal trays or in glass casserole dishes.

3. Place the trays on *top* of the covered solar box cooker or in the panel cooker *without* using an oven cooking bag, as described in step 3 for Sun-Dried Fruits and Vegetables. Cover the trays with fine nylon mesh if necessary.
4. Dry to the desired consistency—chewy or crisp.
5. Cool completely. For best quality, double-bag and store leftovers in the refrigerator for up to 6 months or in the freezer for up to 1 year.

Roasted Nuts or Seeds

2 cups

1. Spread evenly on a dark metal tray:
   2 cups any variety shelled nuts
2. Place the uncovered tray in the solar cooker for 2 hours, or until the nuts are light brown.

Baked Almonds

3 cups

1. Toss together in a pot:
   3 cups shelled almonds (or substitute other nuts)
   1 teaspoon olive oil
   ¼ teaspoon coarse salt or salt substitute
2. Cover and place in the solar cooker for 4 hours.

Sweet Trail Snack Mix

12 cups

1. Stir together in a large pan:
   2 tablespoons brown sugar
   2 tablespoons canola oil
   1 tablespoon vanilla extract
   ⅛ teaspoon cayenne pepper
2. Add and mix well:
   10 cups of a mixture of any of the following: ready-to-eat cereals, shelled nuts or seeds, shredded coconut
3. Place the uncovered pan in the solar cooker for 4 hours.

4. Let cool completely; then stir in:
> 1 cup whole dried raisins, blueberries, or cranberries, or any other dried fruit, chopped
>
> 1 cup chocolate or other chips

Savory Trail Snack Mix

12 cups

1. Stir together in a large pan:
> 1 tablespoon chili powder
>
> 2 tablespoons canola oil
>
> 1 teaspoon dried thyme, crumbled
>
> ½ teaspoon salt
>
> ½ teaspoon sugar

2. Add and mix well:
> 12 cups of a mixture of any of the following: ready-to-eat cereals; shelled nuts or seeds; mini pretzels, crackers, bagel chips, or rice cakes; coarsely crumbled tortilla chips; popped corn; chow mein noodles

3. Place the uncovered pan in the solar cooker for 4 hours.

4. Remove from the solar cooker and cool completely; then stir in:
> ½ cup finely grated Parmesan cheese

Poached Eggs

Serves 4

1. Butter 4 ovenproof cups or small bowls. Break 1 egg into each cup.

2. Place the cups inside one large or two small pots. Cover and place in the solar cooker for 45 minutes, or until firm.

Hard-Boiled Eggs

Serves 4

1. Place in a pot:
> 4 eggs in the shell
>
> 3½ cups water, or just enough to cover the eggs

2. Cover and place in the solar cooker for 3 hours.

Vegetables

Corn on the Cob

Serves 4

1. Pick from your garden or choose fresh from a farmers' market:
   4 ears of corn
2. Do not remove the husks. Wipe the corn and place it whole in the solar cooker—on a tray or wire grate in a box cooker, or inside an oven cooking bag in a panel cooker. Enjoy delicately roasted corn on the cob about 1½ hours later.

Baked Potatoes

Serves 6

1. Scrub but do not peel:
   6 large, mature baking potatoes
2. Let them air-dry. Then put them in a large pot. Cover and place it in the solar cooker for 6 hours, or until the potatoes are tender. Fewer potatoes will cook more quickly.

Baked Sweet Potatoes

Serves 6

1. Scrub but do not peel:
   6 large sweet potatoes or yams
2. Let them air-dry. Cut off the tips to keep them from bursting.
3. Place them in a large pot. Cover and place it in the solar cooker for 3 hours, or until the sweet potatoes are tender. Fewer potatoes will cook more quickly.

Easy Vegetables

Serves 6

This recipe is simplicity itself: place some vegetables in a pot and let the sun cook them.
1. Fill a large pot with:
   8 cups of any kind of cleaned fresh vegetables, chopped or sliced

2. Cover and place in the solar cooker until just tender, from 15 minutes to several hours, according to the age, density, and variety of vegetables. Tender new vegetables such as baby peas cook far more quickly than large chunks of dense vegetables such as carrots.
3. These vegetables can be dressed up, either before or after cooking, with any herbs, sauces, or seasonings you like. But try them cooked as is by the sun, with nothing added, to savor their natural flavor.

Cauliflower Parmesan
Serves 6

---

1. Layer in a pot in this order:
    1 head cauliflower, cut into half florets
    1 large sweet onion, very thinly sliced
    ½ cup grated Parmesan cheese
    26 ounces roasted garlic spaghetti sauce
2. Cover and place in the solar cooker for 3 hours.

Scalloped Potatoes
Serves 6

These are easily made in one step from raw potatoes.
1. Layer *half* of these ingredients in an oiled pot in this order:
    5 mature baking potatoes, about 3 pounds total, scrubbed
        but not peeled, and thinly sliced
    5 mushrooms, thinly sliced
    2 tablespoons whole wheat flour
    2 tablespoons minced chives
    2 tablespoons olive oil
    1 teaspoon salt
    ½ teaspoon freshly ground black pepper
    1 cup shredded extra sharp cheddar cheese
    12 ounces evaporated milk
    ½ cup coarse bread crumbs
2. Repeat, layering the rest of the ingredients in the same order.
3. Cover and place in the solar cooker for 5 hours.

Variation: Substitute parsnips or sweet potatoes for all or part of the baking potatoes.

Summer Vegetable Mélange   *Serves 6*

1. Stir together in a pot:
    > 6 cups mixed summer vegetables, such as peas, green
    > beans, summer squash, carrots, bell pepper, scallions,
    > and eggplant, washed and thinly sliced
2. Stir in:
    > 2 cups fresh diced tomatoes, plus juice
    > 1 bunch fresh basil, chopped
    > 2 cloves garlic, minced
    > 2 tablespoons olive oil
    > ½ teaspoon coarse salt, crushed
    > ¼ teaspoon freshly ground black pepper
3. Cover and place in the solar cooker for 2 hours.

Mediterranean Summer Squash   *Serves 6*

1. Slice and place in an oiled pot:
    > 2 to 4 pounds zucchini, crookneck, or other summer
    > squash
2. Stir in:
    > 1 pound fresh ripe tomatoes, diced, plus juice
    > 1 bunch fresh basil, chopped
3. Cover and place in the solar cooker for 2 to 3 hours, or until tender.

Corn Pudding Royale   *Serves 6*

Serve this as a side dish, or cut it into small squares as an appetizer to
serve 10 to 12.
1. Beat together in a large bowl:
    > kernels scraped from 4 ears of fresh corn, or use 3 cups
    > of frozen corn kernels, thawed
    > 2 tablespoons chopped fresh chives or scallions
    > 2 tablespoons chopped fresh basil or parsley
    > 2 seeded jalapeño peppers, fresh or canned, diced

¼ cup medium ground cornmeal
½ cup freshly grated Parmesan cheese
24 ounces evaporated milk
4 eggs, beaten, or 1 cup egg whites
1 tablespoon sugar
½ teaspoon salt
¼ teaspoon ground nutmeg
⅛ teaspoon cayenne pepper

2. Pour the mixture into a large oiled pot.
3. Cover and place in the solar cooker for 2 to 3 hours, or until just firm.

Baked Potato Slices

Serves 6

1. Thinly slice and then spread evenly over the bottom of a large pot:
   6 large baking potatoes, scrubbed but not peeled
2. Sprinkle over the potatoes:
   ¼ teaspoon ground turmeric
3. Pour over the potatoes:
   4 cups chicken broth
4. Cover and place in the solar cooker for 2 to 3 hours; then remove the cover and return the uncovered pot to the solar cooker for 2 to 3 hours longer, or until tender.
5. Before serving, sprinkle over the potatoes and toss to coat:
   1 teaspoon coarse salt, crushed
   ¼ teaspoon freshly ground black pepper
   ¼ cup freshly grated Parmesan cheese
   2 tablespoons freshly chopped chives (optional)

Potato Wedges

Serves 4

1. Scrub but do not peel:
   4 large baking potatoes
   Cut each of the potatoes lengthwise into 8 wedges, and place the wedges in a single layer in a large pot.

2. Sprinkle over the potatoes:
> 2 tablespoons chili powder
> 1 teaspoon coarse salt
> 2 teaspoons extra virgin olive oil

Toss to coat well.
3. Cover and place in the solar cooker for 4 hours.

Baked Potatoes and Tomatoes
Serves 6

1. Layer in a large oiled pot in this order:
> 1½ pounds very thinly sliced young potatoes, scrubbed but not peeled
> 1 scallion, minced
> 1½ pounds ripe fresh tomatoes, thinly sliced, plus juice
> ¼ cup any variety stock or water
> 1 cup grated Parmesan, Romano, or dry Monterey Jack cheese
> 2 tablespoons olive oil
> ½ teaspoon salt
> ¼ teaspoon freshly ground black pepper
2. Cover and place in the solar cooker for 6 to 7 hours.

Baked Winter Squash
Serves 4

1. Cut in half and remove pulp and seeds from:
> 1 large or 2 small winter squashes, such as acorn, turban, or butternut squash, or a small pumpkin
2. Place the halves cut side down in a pot.
3. Cover and place in the solar cooker for 2 to 3 hours, or until tender.
4. Before serving, turn the squash cut side up and drizzle inside the centers:
> 1 tablespoon honey or maple syrup

Thick Tomato Sauce   6 *cups*

Make extra sauce from the summer's bounty of juicy tomatoes.
1. Sauté in a large skillet for 5 minutes, or until tender:
    1 tablespoon olive oil
    1 large onion, finely chopped
    1 eggplant, diced
    8 ounces fresh mushrooms, sliced
    5 cloves garlic, minced
2. Place the sautéed vegetables in a large pot. Add and stir well:
    10 pounds ripe fresh tomatoes, chopped, plus juice
    1 bunch basil, chopped
    6 ounces canned tomato paste
    ¼ cup red wine
    1 teaspoon salt
    1 teaspoon honey
    ¼ teaspoon crushed red pepper flakes
3. Cover and place in the solar cooker for 4 hours.

Bok Choy   *Serves 4*

1. Rinse, drain, and chop into 1-inch pieces:
    1 head bok choy or Napa cabbage
2. Put the cabbage in a covered pan and place it in the solar cooker
    for 1 to 2 hours, or until tender-crisp.
3. Serve with wedges of fresh lemon.

Greens   *Serves 4*

1. Wash thoroughly in cold water:
    2 large bunches (about 2 pounds) kale, mustard, or
    turnip greens
2. Remove stems. Tear or chop leaves coarsely, and place them in a
    pot. Pour over the greens:
    2 cups any variety broth or stock
3. Cover and place in the solar cooker for 5 to 6 hours, or until tender.

4. Stir in before serving:
> **2 tablespoons honey**
> **½ teaspoon salt**
> **¼ teaspoon freshly ground black pepper**

Stuffed Tomatoes   *Serves 6*

1. Halve crosswise:
> **3 large, ripe tomatoes**

Carefully scoop out the insides of the tomatoes. Chop the insides and place them in a medium bowl. Add to the chopped tomato:
> **1 bunch fresh raw spinach, finely chopped**
> **¾ cup grated Parmesan cheese**
> **3 whole scallions, minced**
> **½ teaspoon salt**
> **½ teaspoon dried thyme**

2. Pack the tomato shells with the spinach mixture. Sprinkle over the tops:
> **⅔ cup soft whole wheat bread crumbs**

Dot with:
> **2 tablespoons butter or olive oil**

3. Cover and place in the solar cooker for 1 to 2 hours, or until the tomato shells are tender.

Baked Mushroom Caps   *Serves 4*

1. Remove the stems from and wipe clean:
> **4 large portobello mushrooms**

2. Place the mushroom caps, gill side up, in a large oiled pot.
3. Sprinkle over the caps:
> **3 cloves garlic, chopped**
> **3 tablespoons chopped fresh parsley**
> **½ teaspoon salt**
> **¼ teaspoon freshly ground black pepper**
> **1 tablespoon olive oil**

4. Cover and place in the solar cooker for 1 hour.

Grains

Barley

Serves 4

Dry toasting brings out the naturally nutty flavor of the grain.

1. Rinse, drain, and dry-toast in a skillet until lightly browned:
     1 cup barley
2. Place the barley in a pot with:
     3 cups any variety stock
     ½ teaspoon salt
     ¼ teaspoon freshly ground black pepper
3. Cover and place in the solar cooker for 4 hours.
4. Serve warm.

Variation: Turn any solar-cooked grains or beans into a hearty salad using this simple vinaigrette dressing. Whisk together in a large bowl:
     ¼ cup canola oil
     ¼ cup vinegar (balsamic, red wine, cider, or rice) or lemon juice
     ¼ teaspoon salt
     ¼ teaspoon ground mustard
Add still-warm cooked barley, rice, couscous, kasha, quinoa, beans, lentils, or baked potatoes to the vinaigrette dressing. Let it cool; then stir in any raw or cooked vegetables, cheese, fish, tofu, or meat for an easy meal.

Brown Rice

Serves 4

1. Place in a pot:
     1¾ cups rinsed, drained short-grain brown rice
     1¾ cups water
     ½ teaspoon salt
     1 whole bay leaf (optional)
2. Cover and place in the solar cooker for 3 to 4 hours, or until fluffy. Remove the bay leaf before serving.

Couscous

Serves 4

1. Stir together in a pot:
      2½ cups water
      2¼ cups couscous
      ½ teaspoon salt
2. Cover and place in the solar cooker for 1 hour, or until dry and fluffy.

Kasha (Buckwheat Groats)

Serves 4

1. Dry-toast in a skillet until lightly browned:
      1¼ cups kasha
2. Place the toasted kasha in a pot along with:
      2 cups water
      ½ teaspoon salt
3. Cover and place in the solar cooker for 2 to 3 hours, or until tender.

Polenta (Coarse Cornmeal)

Serves 6

1. Stir together in a pot:
      2 cups coarse or medium ground cornmeal
      2 tablespoons olive or canola oil
      1 teaspoon salt
      ⅛ teaspoon cayenne pepper
2. Pour over the cornmeal mixture and beat until smooth:
      4½ cups boiling water
3. Cover and place in the solar cooker for 4 hours.

Quinoa

Serves 4

This high-protein grain has a nutty flavor and a pleasant consistency.
1. Place in a pot:
      1½ cups quinoa, rinsed and drained
      2½ cups water
      ½ teaspoon salt
2. Cover and place in the solar cooker for 1 hour, or until dry and fluffy.

Scottish Porridge Oats

Serves 4

1. Mix together in a pot:
   1 ½ cups porridge oats (finely ground oats)
   4 cups water
   3 tablespoons brown sugar
   ½ teaspoon salt
   ½ cup raisins (optional)
2. Cover and place in the solar cooker for 1 ½ hours.
3. Serve warm with milk.

Solar Granola

18 servings

Leave this cereal in the solar cooker all day for extra crunchiness.

1. Dry-toast in a large skillet over medium heat until lightly browned:
   2 cups whole wheat flour
   ½ cup rye flour
   1 cup wheat germ
   1 cup flaked coconut
   ½ cup nutritional yeast (high-protein dried, unleavened yeast)
2. Meanwhile, heat in a saucepan just until bubbling:
   1 ½ cups brown sugar
   1 cup canola oil
   ½ cup honey
3. Stir together in a 10- by 13-inch (4-quart) pan:
   8 cups whole rolled oats
   1 cup hulled sunflower seeds
   2 cups any variety chopped nuts
4. Add the flour and sugar mixtures to the oat mixture in the casserole dish and blend thoroughly.
5. Place the uncovered pan in the solar cooker for 6 to 9 hours, or until browned and crunchy.
6. To store, cool completely; then double-bag and keep in the freezer. Serve with milk and any fresh or dried fruit.

Spreads

Spreads made in a solar cooker require no stirring or tending; choose ripe fresh fruit for spreads that turn out perfectly every time.

Strawberry Jam   *3 cups*

1. Stir together in a pot:
   > **4 cups ripe fresh strawberries, cored and coarsely chopped**
   > **2½ cups granulated sugar**
2. Cover and place in the solar cooker for 2 hours.
3. Pour into clean glass jars and let cool completely. The jam will thicken as it cools.
4. Cover and store in the refrigerator for up to 6 months.

Peach Chutney   *3½ cups*

1. Stir together in a pot:
   > **6 ripe fresh peaches, peeled, pitted, and diced**
   > **1 small sweet onion, minced**
   > **¾ cup brown sugar**
   > **¾ cup white vinegar or apple cider**
   > **½ cup raisins**
   > **3 cloves garlic, minced**
   > **¼ teaspoon ground ginger**
2. Cover and place in the solar cooker for 4 to 5 hours.
3. Pour into clean glass jars and let cool completely. The chutney will thicken as it cools.
4. Cover and store in the refrigerator for up to 6 months.

Apple Butter   *3½ cups*

1. Stir together in a pot:
   > **6 Granny Smith apples, peeled, cored, and finely diced**
   > **1½ cups brown sugar**
   > **½ cup apple juice or apple cider**

> 1 teaspoon ground cinnamon
> ¼ teaspoon ground cloves
> ¼ teaspoon ground allspice

2. Cover and place in the solar cooker for 2 to 3 hours, or until the apples are very tender.
3. Purée; then pour the apple butter into clean glass jars and let cool completely.
4. Cover and store in the refrigerator for up to 6 months.

Chunky Applesauce
3½ cups

---

1. Stir together in a pot:
> 6 apples, peeled, cored, and diced
> ⅓ cup brown sugar or ¼ cup honey
> juice of 1 fresh lemon
> ½ teaspoon ground cinnamon
> dash of salt

2. Cover and place in the solar cooker for 2 hours, or until the apples are tender.
3. If you prefer a less chunky consistency, purée the applesauce. Serve warm, at room temperature, or chilled.

Chapter Three

Soups, Stews, and Chilies

Soups

Easy Stock for Soups and Stews

It's easy to make stock when you have the ingredients handy in your freezer. Simply store your everyday food scraps in a large container in the freezer. Some good scraps to save are:

> **celery, carrot, greens, and parsley stems and leaves**
>
> **ends or skins from onions, tomatoes, squash, green beans, and mushrooms**
>
> **meat or poultry bones and shellfish shells**

Use care when adding pepper stems and seeds to your stock; sweet peppers can make stock bitter, and chili peppers can make it too hot. Cabbage parts are tasty but may be too strong. Taste your cooked stock before using it in a recipe; an overly hot or strong-flavored stock can easily be thinned with water.

1. To make stock, place frozen scraps in a large pot. Cover the scraps with water, and place in the solar cooker for several hours.
2. Strain the stock, discarding the solids.
3. Use immediately or store, covered, in the refrigerator for up to 5 days or in the freezer for up to 6 months.

Tomato Vegetable Soup

Serves 4

1. Stir together in a pot:

> **6 cups (48 ounces) tomato juice**
>
> **6 cups any fresh, canned, or frozen vegetables, diced**

½ teaspoon salt
¼ teaspoon curry powder
2. Cover and place in the solar cooker all day.
3. Serve hot or chilled.

Barley Vegetable Soup
Serves 4

This soup is thick and hearty.
1. Mix together in a pot:
   ½ cup barley, washed, drained, and dry-toasted until light brown
   15 ounces canned diced tomatoes
   1 cup fresh green beans, diced
   1 cup corn kernels, fresh or frozen and thawed
   3 carrots, diced
   1 zucchini, diced
   ½ cup salsa
   4½ cups chicken broth or vegetable stock
   ½ teaspoon salt
   1 whole bay leaf
2. Cover and place in the solar cooker all day.
3. Before serving, remove the bay leaf and stir in:
   ⅓ cup freshly grated Parmesan cheese

Winter Squash Soup
Serves 4

1. Sauté in a large skillet over medium heat for 1 minute:
   1 leek, white part only, minced
   Add and cook 5 minutes longer, stirring occasionally:
   1 winter squash (about 2½ pounds), such as small butternut or large acorn squash, peeled, seeded, and cut into 1-inch cubes
2. Stir together in a pot:
   2 ribs celery, minced
   4 cups chicken broth or any variety stock
   1 teaspoon salt

    ¼ teaspoon ground nutmeg
    dash of cayenne pepper
Add the squash mixture and stir well.
3. Cover and place in the solar cooker for 6 to 8 hours.
4. Before serving, stir in:
    12 ounces evaporated milk
5. Purée the soup (optional). Serve warm, at room temperature, or chilled.

Carrot Soup
Serves 4

---

1. Stir together in a pot:
    4½ cups any variety stock
    1 cup orange juice
    1 leek, white and pale green parts only, finely chopped
    1¼ pounds carrots, scrubbed but not peeled, grated
    5 ribs celery, finely chopped
    1 teaspoon salt
    dash of white pepper
2. Cover and place in the solar cooker for 6 to 8 hours.

Summer Soup
Serves 4

This soup can be served warm, at room temperature, or chilled.
1. Stir together in a pot:
    4 medium zucchini (about 1¾ pounds) or other summer squash, finely chopped
    1 large onion, finely chopped
    ¾ pound green beans, finely chopped
    1 cup fresh corn kernels or fresh peas
    2 tablespoons chopped fresh basil
    3 cups any variety stock
    15 ounces canned small pink beans
    1 teaspoon salt
    ¼ teaspoon curry powder
    ¼ teaspoon freshly ground black pepper
2. Cover and place in the solar cooker for 6 to 8 hours.

Zuppa Italiana   *Serves 4*

1. Wash and drain:
      1 pound kale, chard, or mustard greens
   Separate the stems and leaves. Mince the stems and coarsely chop
   the leaves.
2. Place in a large skillet over medium heat:
      1 tablespoon olive oil
   Add the minced stems and:
      3 cloves garlic, minced
   Cook, stirring occasionally, for 5 minutes.
3. Place the chopped leaves and sautéed stems in a pot along with:
      14 ounces chicken broth
      3 cups vegetable stock or water
      30 ounces canned cannellini beans
      ¾ cup couscous
      ¼ teaspoon crushed red pepper flakes
4. Cover and place in the solar cooker for 5 hours.
5. Before serving, stir in:
      ½ teaspoon salt
      ¾ cup finely grated Parmesan cheese

Bean Curd Soup   *Serves 4*

1. Place in a pot:
      28 ounces firm tofu, cubed
      4 cups any variety clear stock
      2 cups fresh or frozen petite peas, thawed and drained
2. Cover and place in the solar cooker for 3 hours.
3. Before serving, stir in:
      1 teaspoon tamari soy sauce
      ½ teaspoon roasted sesame oil

Garbanzo Pumpkin Soup

Serves 4

1. Stir together in a pot:
   > 45 ounces canned garbanzo beans, rinsed and drained
   > 3 cups (24 ounces) tomato juice
   > 15 ounces canned pumpkin
   > 3 carrots, diced
   > 3 cloves garlic, chopped
   > 2 cups any variety stock
   > 2 tablespoons maple syrup or honey
   > ½ teaspoon salt
   > ½ teaspoon crushed red pepper flakes
   > dash of ground nutmeg
2. Cover and place in the solar cooker for 6 to 8 hours.
3. Before serving, stir in:
   > ½ cup finely grated Parmesan cheese
4. Purée the soup and serve warm.

Easy Bean Soup

Serves 4

1. Stir together in a pot:
   > 30 ounces canned pinquito beans plus juice
   > 15 ounces canned diced tomatoes
   > 1 leek, white and pale green parts only, minced
   > 3 cups vegetable stock, chicken broth, or water
   > 2 carrots, grated
   > 2 tablespoons salsa
2. Cover and place in the solar cooker for 4 hours (soup will hold well even if left in the cooker all day).

Tomato Lentil Soup

Serves 6

This is a filling main dish.
1. Stir together in a pot:
   > 1 cup (8 ounces) dried lentils, rinsed and drained
   > 3 cups any variety stock
   > 1½ cups water

>   28 ounces canned diced tomatoes
>   2 medium potatoes, scrubbed but not peeled, diced
>   2 carrots, diced
>   3 ribs celery, diced
>   2 cloves garlic, minced
>   1 whole bay leaf
>   ⅛ teaspoon cayenne pepper
3. Cover and place in the solar cooker all day.
4. Before serving, remove the bay leaf and stir in:
>   1 teaspoon salt

Baked Potato 'n' Leek Soup   *Serves 4*

1. Finely chop and place in a large pot:
>   4 medium baked potatoes (see Baked Potatoes recipe on
>   page 30)
>   1 large leek, white and pale green parts only

Stir in:
>   4 cups beef, chicken, or vegetable stock
>   1 tablespoon olive oil
>   ¾ teaspoon salt
>   ½ teaspoon freshly ground black pepper
2. Cover and bring to a boil on the stove top, then place in the solar
cooker for 6 hours.
3. Stir in:
>   ¼ cup bacon bits
>   12 ounces evaporated milk
>   ½ cup grated cheddar cheese
4. Return to the solar cooker for 30 minutes longer.

Crushed Potato Soup   *Serves 4*

Roasted garlic gives this simple soup big flavor.
1. Stir together in a pot:
>   3 pounds baking potatoes, scrubbed but not peeled, cut
>   into ½-inch cubes
>   1 red, yellow, or green bell pepper, minced

      3 scallions, minced
      8 cloves roasted garlic, minced
      ¼ teaspoon freshly ground black pepper
2. Pour over the potato mixture:
      4 cups any variety stock
3. Cover and place in the solar cooker for 5 hours.
4. Crush the potatoes lightly and stir in before serving:
      1 cup grated sharp cheddar cheese
      1 teaspoon salt

Ginger Chicken Soup

 Serves 4

1. Stir together in a pot:
      1 leek, white part only, minced
      3 ribs celery, minced
      3 cloves garlic, minced
      2-inch-long piece of fresh ginger root, peeled and grated
      1 pound boneless, skinless chicken breasts, cut into 1-inch cubes
      3½ cups any variety stock
      1 tablespoon tamari soy sauce
      1 teaspoon roasted sesame oil
2. Cover and place in the solar cooker for 3 hours.

Red Bean and Sausage Soup

Serves 4

1. Stir together in a pot:
      15 ounces canned small red beans plus juice
      15 ounces canned diced tomatoes
      2 medium potatoes, scrubbed but not peeled, thinly sliced
      1 bunch fresh spinach, finely chopped
      1 scallion, minced
      4 cups any variety stock
      8 ounces pork, beef, or soy sausage, thinly sliced
      ¼ teaspoon hot sauce
2. Cover and place in the solar cooker for 6 to 8 hours.

Cheddar Chowder   *Serves 4*

1. Stir together in a pot:
   - 15 ounces canned creamed corn
   - 2 large baking potatoes, scrubbed but not peeled, diced
   - 2 carrots, scrubbed but not peeled, grated
   - 2 shallots, minced
   - 3 ribs celery, minced or grated
   - ¼ cup chopped fresh parsley
   - 3 cups vegetable or chicken stock
   - ½ teaspoon salt
   - ¼ teaspoon ground nutmeg
   - ⅛ teaspoon cayenne pepper
2. Cover and place in the solar cooker for 6 hours.
3. Before serving, stir in:
   - 2 cups grated extra sharp cheddar cheese

Clam Chowder   *Serves 4*

1. Combine in a pot:
   - 1 leek, white and pale green parts only, minced
   - 2 ribs celery, finely diced
   - 2 ounces pork, beef, or soy bacon, diced
   - 3 medium Yukon Gold potatoes, scrubbed but not peeled, finely diced
   - 4 cups chicken broth, clam juice, or vegetable stock (or any combination of these)
   - 1 teaspoon fresh minced thyme, or ½ teaspoon dried
   - ⅛ teaspoon ground white pepper
2. Cover and place in the solar cooker for 6 to 8 hours.
3. Stir in and heat briefly:
   - 13 ounces canned clams, minced, plus juice
   - 12 ounces evaporated milk
   - 1 teaspoon salt

Fish Soup

1. Sauté in a skillet over medium heat for 3 minutes:
   >1 tablespoon olive oil
   >1 leek, white part only, minced

   Add and cook 3 minutes longer:
   >2 ribs celery, minced

   Turn off heat and stir in:
   >½ cup dry white wine
2. Stir together in a pot:
   >1 pound any skinless, boneless fish, cut into 1-inch cubes
   >2 cups chopped fresh tomatoes or 15 ounces canned diced tomatoes
   >2 cloves garlic, minced
   >1 cup any variety stock
   >½ teaspoon salt
   >¼ teaspoon crushed red pepper flakes

   Add the leek mixture and stir well.
3. Cover and place in the solar cooker for 6 hours.
4. Purée before serving (optional).

Easy Vegetable Beef Soup

1. Stir together in a pot:
   >1½ cups fresh or canned diced tomatoes plus juice
   >4 cups beef broth
   >1 tablespoon honey
   >1 whole bay leaf
   >2 cups diced cooked roast beef
   >2 carrots, grated
   >1 leek, white and pale green parts only, minced
   >3 ribs celery, finely chopped
   >4 cloves garlic, minced
   >dash of hot sauce
2. Cover and place in the solar cooker for 6 hours.

3. Remove the bay leaf and stir in:
    ¾ **cup couscous**
4. Cover and return to the solar cooker for 10 minutes longer.

Stews

Butter Bean Chicken Stew   Serves 4

1. Stir together in a pot:
    > 1 **pound boneless, skinless chicken cut into ½-inch cubes**
    > ½ **cup bulgur (cracked wheat)**
    > 2 **cups any variety stock**
    > ¼ **cup red wine**
    > 30 **ounces canned butter beans or lima beans, rinsed and drained**
    > 2 **carrots, grated**
    > 2 **cloves garlic, minced**
    > 1 **teaspoon salt**
    > ½ **teaspoon ground white pepper**
2. Cover and place in the solar cooker for 3 hours.

Shrimp Jambalaya   Serves 4

1. Stir together in a pot:
    > 1 **onion, chopped**
    > 4 **cloves garlic, minced**
    > 1 **red or green bell pepper, chopped**
    > 1 **carrot, grated**
    > 2 **ribs celery, finely chopped**
    > 3 **cups spaghetti sauce**
    > ½ **cup chopped fresh parsley**
    > 1 **pound large, whole uncooked shrimp, peeled and deveined**

> ½ cup uncooked orzo or riso pasta
> 1½ cups any variety stock or water
> ½ teaspoon chopped fresh thyme, or ¼ teaspoon dried
> ¼ teaspoon crushed red pepper flakes
> ¼ teaspoon freshly ground black pepper
> ¼ teaspoon salt

2. Cover and place in the solar cooker for 5 hours.

Bean and Eggplant Stew   Serves 4

1. Sauté in a skillet over medium heat for 5 minutes:
   > 1 tablespoon olive oil
   > 1 onion, diced
   > 1 medium eggplant, chopped
2. Stir together in a pot:
   > 30 ounces canned cannellini beans, rinsed and drained
   > 15 ounces canned diced tomatoes plus juice
   > 1 tablespoon minced fresh basil, or 1 teaspoon dried
   > 1 teaspoon salt
   > 1 teaspoon sugar
   > ½ teaspoon freshly ground black pepper

   Stir in the eggplant mixture.
3. Cover and place in the solar cooker for 5 hours.

Vegetable Stew   Serves 4

1. Sauté in a large skillet over medium heat for 12 to 15 minutes, or until fragrant:
   > 1 tablespoon olive oil
   > 1 large onion, chopped
   > 3 button mushrooms, quartered, or 1 small portobello mushroom cut into 1-inch cubes
   > 1½ pounds Yukon Gold potatoes, scrubbed but not peeled, cut into 1-inch cubes

2. Place the sautéed vegetables in a pot. Stir in:
> 1 large acorn squash or 1 small butternut squash, peeled, seeded, and cut into 2-inch cubes
>
> 2 cloves garlic, minced
>
> 2 cups any variety broth or stock
>
> ½ cup dry white wine
>
> ⅓ cup tamari soy sauce
>
> ½ cup TVP (textured vegetable protein)
>
> 1 teaspoon salt
>
> ½ teaspoon freshly ground black pepper
>
> ¼ teaspoon crushed red pepper flakes

3. Cover and place in the solar cooker for 5 hours.

Seafood Stew   Serves 4

1. Sauté in a skillet over medium heat for 3 minutes:
> 1 tablespoon olive oil
>
> 1 leek, white and pale green parts only, finely chopped

2. Place the leek in a pot and stir in:
> 1½ pounds baking potatoes, scrubbed but not peeled, cut into ½-inch cubes
>
> 1 pound boneless fish fillets, cut into ½-inch cubes; whole mussels; whole shelled shrimp; or any combination of these
>
> 3 cups chicken broth
>
> ¼ cup dry white wine
>
> ½ teaspoon salt
>
> ½ teaspoon freshly ground black pepper

3. Cover and place in the solar cooker for 5 hours.

Chilies and Beans

Basic Beans
Serves 6

1. Soak overnight in the refrigerator in a covered dark enamel pot:
   2 cups dried pinto beans, washed and sorted
   6 cups water
2. First thing in the morning, remove the beans and water from the refrigerator. Stir in:
   1 teaspoon ground cumin
3. Cover and place in the solar cooker all day.
4. Stir in before serving:
   1 tablespoon chili powder
   1 teaspoon salt
5. Serve with tortillas, rice, or noodles and hot sauce (optional).

Tip: To cook dried beans on low-sun days, bring the beans and water to a boil on your kitchen range or camp stove before placing them in the solar cooker.

Basic Lentils
Serves 6

1. Place in a large pot:
   2 cups dried lentils, rinsed and drained
   6 cups water
   ½ dried bay leaf
2. Cover and place in the solar cooker for 3 to 4 hours.
3. Remove bay leaf. Stir in before serving:
   1 teaspoon salt
   ¼ teaspoon freshly ground black pepper
   dash of hot sauce

Quick Chili Beans
Serves 4

1. Stir together in a pot:
   30 ounces any variety canned beans, rinsed and drained
   28 ounces canned diced tomatoes plus juice
   2 tablespoons taco seasoning
2. Cover and place in the solar cooker for 1½ hours.
3. Serve with rice or tortillas.

Drunken Beans
Serves 6 to 8

1. Heat in a skillet over medium-low heat:
   1 teaspoon olive oil
   When the oil is hot, add and cook for 10 minutes:
   1 onion, finely chopped
   3 carrots, grated
   3 ribs celery, finely chopped
   Add and cook 3 minutes longer:
   4 cloves garlic, minced
   1 tablespoon brown sugar
   1 teaspoon salt
   ½ teaspoon ground cumin
2. Place the cooked vegetables in a large pot and stir in:
   53 ounces canned pinto beans, rinsed and drained
   28 ounces canned crushed tomatoes plus juice
   12 ounces dark beer
   1 tablespoon hot sauce
3. Cover and place in the solar cooker for 5 to 6 hours.
4. Serve with rice or tortillas.

Chili Mac
Serves 4

1. Sauté in a skillet over medium heat for 5 to 8 minutes, or until soft:
   1 tablespoon olive oil
   1 onion, diced
   1 bell pepper, diced

2. Meanwhile, stir together in a pot:
      1 cup uncooked small elbow macaroni
      26 ounces spaghetti sauce
      30 ounces canned pinto beans plus juice
      3 jalapeño peppers, fresh or canned, minced
      2 ounces pepperoni or soy pepperoni, thinly sliced
      1 teaspoon salt
3. Stir in the sautéed onion mixture.
4. Cover and place in the solar cooker for 3 hours.
5. Before serving, stir in:
      1 cup shredded cheddar cheese

Fun Beans
Serves 4

1. Stir together in a pot:
      2 medium zucchini, diced
      4 carrots, grated
      2 cloves garlic, minced
      15 ounces canned diced tomatoes
      1 cup apple cider or apple juice
      30 ounces canned cannellini beans, rinsed and drained
      ½ teaspoon salt
      ¼ teaspoon hot sauce
2. Cover and place in the solar cooker for 6 hours.
3. Before serving, stir in:
      ½ cup pork or soy bacon bits
      ½ cup grated Parmesan cheese
4. Serve with tortillas or tortilla chips.

Chili Con Carne
Serves 4

1. Sauté in a skillet over medium heat for 8 minutes:
      1 teaspoon olive oil
      1 onion, diced

    1 red bell pepper, diced
    1¼ pounds lean ground beef, turkey, or soy
  Stir in and cook 2 minutes longer:
    2 teaspoons chili powder
    1 teaspoon salt
    ⅛ teaspoon cayenne pepper
2. Stir together in a pot:
    15 ounces canned pinto beans, rinsed and drained
    28 ounces whole peeled tomatoes plus juice
    6 ounces tomato paste
  Stir in the sautéed meat mixture.
3. Cover and place in the solar cooker for 4 hours.

Chili Beans Plus
Serves 4

1. Sauté in a skillet over medium heat for 5 minutes:
    1 tablespoon olive oil
    1 large onion, minced
    3 cloves garlic, minced
  Add and sauté 1 minute longer:
    1 red bell pepper, diced
    1 tablespoon chili powder
    1 teaspoon ground cumin
    1 teaspoon dried oregano
    1 teaspoon ground mustard
    1 teaspoon salt
2. Stir together in a pot:
    1 whole bay leaf
    30 ounces canned pinto beans, rinsed and drained
    30 ounces diced tomatoes plus juice
    ½ cup any variety stock
    14 ounces sausage-style soy ground round, crumbled
3. Stir in the sautéed onion mixture. Cover and place in the solar cooker for 6 hours.
4. Remove the bay leaf, and serve with rice or some other grain.

Bean Bake

Serves 4 to 6

1. Sauté in a skillet over medium heat for 5 minutes:
   - 1 teaspoon olive oil
   - 1 large onion, finely chopped
2. Meanwhile, stir together in a pot:
   - 16 ounces canned baked beans (vegetarian or pork and beans)
   - 16 ounces canned lima or garbanzo beans
   - 16 ounces canned kidney beans
   - 16 ounces diced tomatoes
   - ½ cup TVP (textured vegetable protein)
   - ⅓ cup brown sugar
   - 2 tablespoons cider vinegar
   - 1 tablespoon ground mustard
   - ½ teaspoon cayenne pepper
   - 3 slices pork, beef, or soy bacon, finely chopped
   - 1 teaspoon liquid smoke

   Add the sautéed onion and mix well.
3. Cover and place in the solar cooker for 6 hours.
4. Serve with any grain.

Sloppy Josies

Serves 4

1. Heat in a large skillet over medium heat:
   - 1 tablespoon canola oil

   Add and cook, stirring occasionally, for 5 minutes:
   - 1 small onion, diced
   - 1 bell pepper, diced
   - 1 pound ground turkey, beef, or soy
2. Meanwhile, stir together in a pot:
   - 14 ounces canned diced tomatoes
   - 1 cup water
   - ¼ cup red wine
   - 1 dill pickle, diced
   - 1 tablespoon ground mustard
   - 1 tablespoon chili powder

1 tablespoon cider vinegar
1 tablespoon tamari soy sauce
1 tablespoon honey

3. Stir in the meat mixture. Place in the solar cooker for 6 to 8 hours.
4. Serve on:

4 split and toasted hamburger buns

Black Bean Vegetable Chili   *Serves 4*

1. Stir together in a pot:

4 cloves garlic, minced
6 cups finely chopped vegetables such as peas, onions,
   summer squash, and green beans
15 ounces canned black beans, rinsed and drained
4 ounces canned diced medium or hot green chilies, plus
   juice
1 cup chopped fresh or canned, drained tomatoes
¾ cup TVP (textured vegetable protein)
3 tablespoons chili powder
1 tablespoon brown sugar
½ teaspoon salt
2 cups tomato juice or any variety stock

2. Cover and place in the solar cooker for 6 to 8 hours.
3. Serve with any grain.

CHAPTER FOUR

MAIN DISHES

Casseroles and Other Main Courses

Cheese Strata
Serves 4

This is a good choice for partly cloudy days because it cooks quickly.

1. Beat together in a large bowl:

    6 eggs or 1½ cups egg whites

    24 ounces evaporated milk

    1 cup cottage cheese

    ¾ cup freshly grated Parmesan cheese

    3 whole scallions, finely chopped

    ¼ cup chopped parsley

    1 teaspoon salt

    1 teaspoon minced fresh rosemary leaves, or ½ teaspoon dried

    ⅛ teaspoon cayenne pepper

2. Stir in until saturated:

    8-ounce sourdough baguette, cut into 1-inch cubes (or use about 4 cups of any cubed white or light wheat bread)

3. Pour the mixture into an oiled pot. Cover and place in the solar cooker for 1 to 2 hours, or until just firm. Although this dish cooks quickly, it will hold all day in the solar cooker.

y Chicken

Serves 6

h is simple but sumptuous.

e in a clean paper bag:

>   ¼ cup whole wheat flour
>   1 teaspoon dried thyme
>   1½ pounds chicken tenders

ose the bag tightly and shake vigorously to coat the chicken.

ce the chicken tenders in a single layer in a large, shallow pot.

rinkle evenly over the chicken:

>   1 ounce (1 packet) dried onion soup mix
>   ½ pound fresh mushrooms, thinly sliced or chopped

ur over the chicken:

>   24 ounces evaporated milk

Cover and place in the solar cooker for 3 hours, or until the internal temperature of the chicken pieces reaches 165 degrees; use a probe thermometer to check.

Serve with rice (see Brown Rice recipe on page 37) or noodles (see Basic Pasta recipe on page 81).

e-Step Chicken Cacciatore

Serves 4

Stir together in a pot:

>   2 cloves garlic, minced
>   6 large mushrooms, very coarsely chopped
>   28 ounces canned peeled Italian plum tomatoes, coarsely chopped, plus juice
>   6 ounces tomato paste
>   ¼ cup dry sherry
>   ½ teaspoon salt
>   ½ teaspoon freshly ground black pepper
>   ½ teaspoon dried thyme
>   ½ teaspoon dried oregano
>   1¼ pounds chicken tenders, cut into 1-inch cubes

2. Cover and place in the solar cooker for 3 hours, or until the internal temperature of the chicken pieces reaches 165 degrees; check with a probe thermometer.

Meatloaf

1. Mix together in a large bowl:
   - 30 ounces canned garbanzo beans, mashed
   - 2 eggs, beaten, or ½ cup egg whites
   - 1 pound ground beef, pork, or soy
   - 1 cup rolled oats
   - 3 shallots, finely chopped
   - 1 bell pepper, finely chopped
   - 3 cloves garlic, minced
   - ¼ cup pork or soy bacon bits
   - 1 tablespoon Worcestershire sauce
   - ½ teaspoon salt
   - ⅛ teaspoon cayenne pepper
2. Shape the mixture into a wide, shallow loaf, and inch-diameter pot.
3. Pour over the loaf:
   - ½ cup salsa
4. Cover and place in the solar cooker for 5 hours.
5. Serve with baked potatoes or rice.

Cream

This dis
1. Pla

Cl
Pl
2. S

3. P

4. (

5.

O

1.

Easy Cassoulet

1. Stir together in a pot:
   - 15 ounces canned cannellini beans, rinsed an
   - 15 ounces canned diced tomatoes plus juice
   - ¼ cup quick-cooking grits
   - 3 cups chicken broth or any variety stock
   - 13 ounces fully cooked spicy sausage, such as li chorizo, sliced
   - 3 ribs celery, diced
   - 3 cloves garlic, minced
   - 1 bell pepper, chopped
   - ½ teaspoon crushed red pepper flakes
   - ½ teaspoon minced fresh thyme, or ¼ teaspoon dr
2. Cover and place in the solar cooker for 6 hours.

Easy Pot Roast with Potatoes   *Serves 6 to 8*

1. Distribute evenly over the bottom of a large oiled pot:
    8 small Yukon Gold potatoes, scrubbed but not peeled, quartered
2. Place on top of the potatoes:
    2- to 3-pound piece of chuck-eye, top round, or other beef roast
3. Sprinkle over the meat and potatoes:
    1 ounce (1 packet) dried onion soup mix
    2 tablespoons Italian seasoning
4. Cover and place in the solar cooker for 6 hours, or until a probe thermometer inserted into the center of the roast reaches 145 degrees.

Portobello Mushroom Burgers   *Serves 4*

1. To make the marinade, whisk together in a small bowl:
    2 tablespoons extra virgin olive oil
    2 tablespoons balsamic vinegar
    ¼ teaspoon salt
    ¼ teaspoon dried thyme
    ⅛ teaspoon ground mustard
    Set aside.
2. Gently wipe clean and slice the stems from:
    4 large portobello mushrooms
3. Place the mushrooms, gill side down, in a large pot. Drizzle half the marinade over the tops of the mushrooms. Then turn them gill side up and drizzle the other half of the marinade over the bottoms.
4. Cover and place in the solar cooker for 1 hour, or until tender.
5. Place on plates:
    4 hamburger buns
    Spread over the opened buns:
    ½ cup fresh whole basil leaves
6. Place the mushrooms on the buns and serve warm.

Polenta Squares with Vegetable Sauce   *Serves 4 to 6*

1. Prepare polenta (see the recipe on page 38).
2. Meanwhile, place in a pot:

> **8 cups fresh, or frozen and thawed, chopped vegetables, such as summer squash, broccoli, green beans, eggplant, cauliflower, or kale**
> **3 cups spaghetti sauce**

3. Cover and place in the solar cooker for 3 hours.
4. To serve, slice the cooked polenta into 4 to 6 pieces and place them in individual bowls. Sprinkle over the polenta:

> **¾ cup freshly grated Parmesan cheese**

Pour the vegetable sauce over the polenta.

Mexican Corn Bake   *Serves 4*

1. Stir together in a pot:

> **3 eggs, beaten, or ¾ cup egg whites**
> **15 ounces canned pinto beans, rinsed and drained**
> **15 ounces frozen or canned whole kernel corn, rinsed and drained**
> **15 ounces canned diced tomatoes, drained**
> **½ cup salsa**
> **1 bell pepper, diced**
> **2 ribs celery, diced**
> **3 cloves garlic, minced**
> **1 cup shredded mozzarella cheese**
> **½ cup grated Parmesan cheese**
> **2 tablespoons chili powder**
> **1 tablespoon sugar**
> **½ teaspoon salt**

2. Cover and place in the solar cooker for 3 to 4 hours.

Layered Vegetable Casserole
Serves 4

1. Spread *half* of the following ingredients in an oiled pot in this order:
   4 large Yukon Gold potatoes, scrubbed but not peeled, thinly sliced
   1 cup plain yogurt
   15 ounces canned garbanzo beans, rinsed and drained
   1 onion, diced
   1 bunch fresh basil, chopped
   ½ cup roasted red bell pepper strips, drained
   1 cup shredded Monterey Jack cheese
   1 teaspoon salt
   2 cups chicken broth
2. Repeat, layering the rest of the ingredients.
3. Cover and place in the solar cooker for 6 hours.

Green Frittata
Serves 4

1. Sauté for 2 minutes in a large skillet over medium heat:
   1 teaspoon olive oil
   4 whole scallions, minced
   Add and cook 5 minutes longer:
   1 bunch spinach, finely chopped
   10 medium-sized mushrooms, thinly sliced
2. Remove from heat and stir in:
   ½ cup minced parsley
3. Beat together in a large bowl:
   5 eggs or 1¼ cups egg whites
   1 cup yogurt
   1 cup finely grated Parmesan cheese
   ½ teaspoon salt
   ¼ teaspoon freshly ground black pepper
   Add the spinach mixture and blend well.
4. Pour into an oiled pan, cover, and place in the solar cooker for 6 hours.

Solar Egg Rolls

Serves 4

1. Chop in a food processor or mix together in a large bowl:
    > **14 ounces firm tofu, crumbled**
    > **1 tablespoon tamari soy sauce**
    > **1 teaspoon roasted sesame oil**
    > **1 teaspoon salt**
    > **⅛ teaspoon crushed red pepper flakes**
    > **2-inch piece of fresh ginger root, peeled and finely
    >   chopped**
    > **4 scallions, minced**
    > **1 bunch fresh raw spinach or 1 small Napa cabbage,
    >   finely chopped**
    > **1 red or yellow bell pepper, diced**
2. Spread on the counter:
    > **12 egg roll wrappers, 6 by 7 inches**
3. Spread the tofu mixture in a line down the centers of the wrappers.
4. Fold the sides of the wrappers inward, roll them up tightly, and
    place them seam side down in an oiled pot.
5. To make the sauce, stir together in a small bowl:
    > **¾ cup roasted garlic cloves (18 cloves), chopped**
    > **2 tablespoons granulated sugar**
    > **3 tablespoons rice vinegar**
    > **1 teaspoon roasted sesame oil**
6. Spread the sauce evenly over the rolled wrappers.
7. Cover and place in the solar cooker for 1½ to 2 hours.
8. Serve with rice.

Summer Vegetable Casserole

Serves 4

Use your extra summer squash in this tasty casserole.
1. Stir together in a pot:
    > **4 eggs, beaten, or 1 cup egg whites**
    > **2 tablespoons extra virgin olive oil**
    > **1 large fresh tomato, diced**
    > **1 bell pepper, diced**

7 cups any variety raw summer squash, coarsely grated
2 fresh jalapeño peppers, seeded and minced
2 shallots, minced
1 cup whole wheat flour
1½ cups shredded sharp cheddar cheese
½ cup pesto sauce
1 teaspoon coarse salt
⅛ teaspoon cayenne pepper

2. Cover and place in the solar cooker for 3 hours, or until just firm.

Mushroom Quiche
Serves 4

1. Beat together in a large bowl:
   3 eggs or ¾ cup egg whites
   12 ounces evaporated milk
   1 cup shredded Gruyère cheese
   1 pound any variety tofu
   3 scallions, white and pale green parts only, minced
   8 ounces fresh mushrooms, finely diced
   1 teaspoon salt
   ½ teaspoon minced fresh thyme, or ¼ teaspoon dried
   ¼ teaspoon ground white pepper
   ⅛ teaspoon ground nutmeg

2. Pour into an oiled pot. Cover and place in the solar cooker for 4 hours, or until firm. This quiche will hold in the solar cooker all day.

Cottage Melt
Serves 4

1. Beat together in a large bowl:
   4 eggs or 1 cup egg whites
   3 tablespoons extra virgin olive oil
   12 ounces (1½ cups) cottage cheese
   ¾ cup finely grated Parmesan cheese
   1 bunch fresh raw spinach, finely chopped
   1 bunch fresh basil, finely chopped

¼ **cup whole wheat flour**
¼ **teaspoon salt**
¼ **teaspoon freshly ground black pepper**

2. Pour the mixture into an oiled pot. Cover and place in the solar cooker for 4 hours, or until firm.

Eggplant Parmesan
Serves 4

There is no need to fry or parboil the eggplant. Assemble this dish in the morning, and leave it in the solar cooker all day for tender, tasty eggplant.

1. Have ready:
    3½ **cups roasted garlic spaghetti sauce**
    1 **large eggplant, about** 1¼ **pounds, cut into** ¼-**inch-thick slices**
    1½ **cups fresh or thawed frozen peas**
    1 **cup shredded mozzarella cheese**
    ½ **cup freshly grated Parmesan cheese**

2. Spread in a large oiled pot:
    ½ **cup of the spaghetti sauce**

3. Layer the rest of the ingredients in the pot in the following order: half the sliced eggplant, half the peas, half the mozzarella cheese, half the remaining spaghetti sauce, and half the Parmesan cheese.

4. Repeat with the other half of the ingredients.

5. Sprinkle over the top:
    1 **tablespoon chopped fresh oregano, or** 1 **teaspoon dried**
    ½ **teaspoon freshly ground black pepper**
    ½ **cup water**

6. Cover and place in the solar cooker all day.

Cashew Curry

Serves 4

1. Heat a large skillet over medium-low heat and add:
    1 tablespoon roasted sesame oil
    When the oil is hot, add and cook for 5 minutes:
        5 cups any chopped fresh vegetables, such as onion, cabbage, carrots, broccoli, green beans, and mushrooms
    Stir in and cook 3 minutes longer:
    ½ cup cashews
    1 tablespoon curry powder
    1 teaspoon ground turmeric
    1 teaspoon salt
    ¼ teaspoon cayenne pepper
2. Place the vegetable mixture in a pot. Stir in:
    28 ounces canned crushed tomatoes
    3 cups any variety stock
    1½ cups couscous
    ½ cup TVP (textured vegetable protein)
3. Cover and place in the solar cooker for 4 hours, or until the vegetables are tender.

Stuffed Roll Sandwiches

Serves 4

1. To make the filling, blend together in a large bowl:
    8 ounces sharp cheddar cheese, shredded
    2 bell peppers, finely chopped
    4 whole scallions, finely chopped
    4 cups baby spinach leaves, finely chopped
    2 tablespoons olive oil
    ¼ teaspoon salt
    ¼ teaspoon freshly ground black pepper
2. Slice partially through lengthwise:
    4 sourdough rolls, 6 inches long
3. Stuff the filling into the rolls, and place them in a pot.
4. Cover and place in the solar cooker for 1 to 1½ hours.

Fish and Seafood

Salsa Fish
Serves 4

This is an incredibly easy way to cook fish.
1. Place skin side down in a single layer in an oiled pot:
    4 fish fillets
    Pour evenly over the fillets:
    ¾ cup mild, medium, or hot salsa
2. Cover and place in the solar cooker for 2 to 3 hours, or until the fish flakes easily with a fork.
3. Serve with rice or some other grain.

"Marinated" Fish Fillets
Serves 4

The solar cooker marinates and cooks your fish fillets in one step.
1. Place in an oiled pot:
    4 thick, boneless fish fillets
2. Mix together in a small bowl:
    2 tablespoons tamari soy sauce
    1 tablespoon dry sherry or fruit juice
    1 teaspoon roasted sesame oil
    1-inch piece of fresh ginger root, peeled and minced
    ½ teaspoon crushed red pepper flakes
3. Spread the soy sauce mixture evenly over the fillets.
4. Cover and place in the solar cooker for 2 to 3 hours, or until the fish flakes easily with a fork.

Fish and Vegetables
Serves 4 to 6

1. Stir together in a pot:
    1¾ pounds boneless fish fillets, cut into 1-inch cubes
    1 onion, thinly sliced

1 red bell pepper, cut into 1-inch squares
4 medium zucchini, cut into 1-inch cubes
2 cloves garlic, minced
45 ounces canned diced tomatoes plus juice
1 bunch basil, minced
1 teaspoon salt
½ teaspoon pepper
½ cup dry white wine

2. Cover and place in the solar cooker for 4 hours.
3. Serve with rice or pasta.

Fish Gratin   *Serves 4*

1. Beat together in a medium bowl:
   2 eggs or ½ cup egg whites
   1 cup milk
   2 shallots, minced
   ¼ cup whole wheat flour
   ½ teaspoon salt
   ½ teaspoon Old Bay seasoning
2. Measure out:
   2 cups bread or cracker crumbs or crushed corn flakes
   Sprinkle *half* the crumbs evenly over the bottom of a large oiled pot.
3. Place in a single layer over the crumbs in the pot:
   1 pound boneless, skinless fish fillets
4. Pour the milk mixture over the fish.
5. Sprinkle the remaining crumbs evenly over the top. On top of the crumbs, sprinkle:
   ½ cup freshly grated Parmesan cheese
6. Cover and place in the solar cooker for 1½ to 2 hours, or until the fish flakes easily with a fork.
7. Serve with rice or other grains or potatoes.

Curried Fish Fillets

Serves 4

1. Grind together in a food processor or blender:
    2-inch piece of fresh ginger root, peeled
    5 cloves garlic
    ¼ teaspoon salt
    dash of cayenne pepper
    dash of ground cumin
2. Stir in:
    1¼ cups plain yogurt
3. Place in a single layer in an oiled pot:
    4 boneless fish fillets
4. Spread the yogurt mixture over the fillets.
5. Cover and place in the solar cooker for 2 to 3 hours, or until the fish flakes easily with a fork.
6. Serve with rice or other grains.

Pecan Salmon

Serves 4

1. Place in an oiled pot:
    4 salmon steaks, about 1½ inches thick
2. Mix together in a small bowl:
    2 tablespoons olive oil
    3 tablespoons honey
    2 tablespoons balsamic vinegar
    1 cup chopped pecans
    ½ teaspoon coarse salt
    ½ teaspoon freshly ground black pepper
3. Spread the mixture evenly over the steaks.
4. Cover and place in the solar cooker for 2 hours, or until the fish flakes easily with a fork.

Salmon Loaf

Serves 4

1. Stir together in a large bowl:
   > 3 eggs, beaten, or ¾ cup egg whites
   > ½ cup milk
   > 15 ounces canned salmon, drained and flaked
   > 2 cups bread or cracker crumbs
   > 1 cup shredded sharp cheddar cheese
   > 4 whole scallions, minced
   > 2 ribs celery, minced
   > 2 tablespoons Old Bay seasoning
2. Oil an 8-by-8-inch casserole dish. Spread the salmon mixture in the dish, and place the uncovered dish in the solar cooker for 2 hours.
3. After 2 hours, pour over the loaf:
   > 2 cups spaghetti sauce
4. Return it to the solar cooker for 30 minutes longer.

Crab Parmesan

Serves 4

1. Beat together in a large bowl:
   > 4 eggs or 1 cup egg whites
   > 12 ounces evaporated milk
   > 1 cup freshly grated Parmesan or Romano cheese
   > 2 pounds crabmeat or imitation crab, flaked
   > 1 teaspoon olive oil
   > 1 red bell pepper, minced
   > 3 scallions, white parts only, minced
   > 2 ribs celery, diced
   > 1 teaspoon Old Bay seasoning
   > ¾ teaspoon salt
   > ⅛ teaspoon cayenne pepper
2. Pour the mixture into an oiled pot. Cover and place in the solar cooker for 2 hours, or until just firm. Although this dish cooks quickly, it will hold all day in the solar cooker.

Baked Crab Cakes

Serves 4 (8 cakes)

1. Beat together in a large bowl:
    > **1 egg or ¼ cup egg whites**
    > **¼ cup mayonnaise**
    > **1 teaspoon ground mustard**
    > **1 teaspoon dried thyme**
    > **½ teaspoon hot sauce**
    > **2 whole scallions, minced**
    > **1 tablespoon minced parsley**
    > **1 pound crabmeat or imitation crab, flaked**
2. Coarsely crush:
    > **1 cup saltine crackers (about 23 crackers)**

    Stir ¾ cup of the crushed crackers into the crab mixture.
3. Shape the mixture into 8 cakes; then roll them in the remaining ¼ cup of crushed crackers.
4. Place the cakes in a single layer in an oiled pot. Spray the tops of the cakes with olive or canola oil.
5. Cover and place in the solar cooker for 2 hours.
6. Serve with rice or other grains and this sauce (optional):
    > **4 tablespoons plain yogurt, sour cream, or mayonnaise**
    > **2 tablespoons pickle relish**

Crab Strata

Serves 4

1. Beat together in a large bowl:
    > **6 eggs or 1½ cups egg whites**
    > **24 ounces (3 cups) evaporated milk**
    > **1 pound crabmeat or imitation crab, flaked**
    > **1 cup shredded Monterey Jack cheese**
    > **4 ounces fresh mushrooms, thinly sliced**
    > **4 cloves garlic, minced**
    > **1 teaspoon salt**
    > **¼ teaspoon ground white pepper**
2. Stir in until saturated:
    > **3 cups cubed bread (about 3 slices)**

3. Pour into an oiled pot. Cover and place in the solar cooker for 2 hours, or until firm.

Enchiladas

Versatile Enchiladas

Serves 4

These are sassy and can have a different taste every time you make them by varying the main ingredient of the filling.
1. To make the filling, stir together in a large bowl:
> **1 pound cooked diced beef, lamb, chicken, or turkey; or crumbled tofu**
> **2 cups plain yogurt or sour cream**
> **2 cups any variety shredded cheese**
> **1 tablespoon taco seasoning**
2. Lay out on the counter:
> **8 whole-grain tortillas, 8-inch diameter**
> Spread the filling mixture evenly over the tortillas. Roll them up, turning the sides inward as you roll, and lay them seam side down in a single layer in an oiled pot.
3. Spread evenly over the enchiladas:
> **1 cup mild, medium, or hot salsa**
4. Cover and place in the solar cooker for 2 hours. Let stand outside the cooker for 5 minutes before serving.

Easy Enchiladas

Serves 4 to 6

1. Lay out on the counter:
> **12 tortillas, 8-inch diameter**
> Distribute evenly over the centers of the tortillas:
> **2 pounds ricotta cheese**
> **1 onion, diced**
> **1 bell pepper, diced**
2. Roll the tortillas, turning the sides inward as you roll, and place them in a single layer in an oiled pot.

3. Pour evenly over the enchiladas:
     28 ounces canned mild green enchilada sauce
4. Cover and place in the solar cooker for 2 hours.

Creamy Crab Enchiladas

Serves 4

1. Mix together in a large bowl:
     1 pound crabmeat or imitation crab, flaked
     1 pound ricotta cheese
     ½ cup grated Parmesan cheese
     2 teaspoons Old Bay seasoning
     ¼ teaspoon cayenne pepper
2. Lay out on the counter:
     8 tortillas, 8-inch diameter
   Spread the crab mixture evenly over the tortillas. Roll them up, turning the sides inward as you roll, and place them in a single layer, seam side down, in an oiled pot.
3. Spread evenly over the enchiladas:
     1 cup spaghetti sauce
4. Cover and place in the solar cooker for 2 to 3 hours.

Vegetable Enchiladas

Serves 4 to 6

1. Lay out on the counter:
     12 tortillas, 8-inch diameter
2. Spread evenly over the tortillas:
     5 cups any variety cooked, chopped vegetables, fresh,
        canned, or frozen
3. Sprinkle evenly over the vegetables:
     1 tablespoon chili powder
     1 pound any variety cheese, diced or shredded
4. Roll up the tortillas, turning the sides inward as you roll. Then place them, seam side down, in a single layer in an oiled pot.
5. Pour evenly over the enchiladas:
     32 ounces (4 cups) spaghetti sauce
6. Cover and place in the solar cooker for 2 hours.

Portobello Mushroom Stacked Enchiladas

Serves 6 to 8

1. To make the filling, stir together in a large bowl:
   2 portobello mushrooms, about ½ pound total, diced
   1 pound fresh mozzarella cheese, diced
   1 bunch fresh raw spinach, coarsely chopped
   2 fresh jalapeño chilies, seeded and minced
2. Have ready:
   6 tortillas or whole-grain wraps, 10-inch diameter
3. Place 1 tortilla in the center of a large oiled pot. Spread ¾ cup of the filling evenly over the entire tortilla. Top with a second tortilla and filling. Repeat until all the tortillas and filling are used.
4. Pour evenly over the top:
   28 ounces roasted garlic spaghetti sauce
5. Cover and place in the solar cooker for 2 hours.
6. Slice into wedges to serve.

Variation: Substitute 2 cups cooked diced chicken for the mushrooms.

Cheddar Chilies Rellenos

Serves 4

There is no need to remove the pepper skins; the solar cooker will make them tender.

1. Cut in half lengthwise, core, and seed:
   6 mild chili peppers, such as Anaheim
2. Fill the chilies with:
   4 cloves garlic, minced
   16 ounces refried beans
   1½ cups cubed or crumbled sharp cheddar cheese
   Set the chilies in a single layer in an oiled pot.
3. Beat together in a large bowl:
   8 eggs or 2 cups egg whites
   24 ounces (3 cups) evaporated milk
   4 tablespoons whole wheat flour
   1 teaspoon salt
   ½ teaspoon cayenne pepper

4. Pour the egg mixture over the chilies. Cover and place in the solar cooker for 6 hours.

Variation: If fresh mild chili peppers are unavailable, use small sweet peppers and sprinkle 1 teaspoon crushed dried red pepper flakes over them before filling.

Lasagna

Red Lasagna
Serves 4

1. In an oiled pot, layer *half* of these ingredients in this order:
   6 uncooked, oven-ready lasagna noodles
   3 fresh mushrooms, finely sliced
   ½ cup TVP (textured vegetable protein)
   1 pound ricotta cheese
   ¾ cup pesto sauce
   26 ounces roasted garlic spaghetti sauce
   1 cup roasted sweet red peppers, drained and chopped
   ¾ cup water
2. Repeat the layers using the rest of the ingredients.
3. Cover and place in the solar cooker for 6 hours.

White Lasagna
Serves 4

1. Sauté in a large skillet over medium heat until light brown:
   1 small onion, diced
   1 pound ground beef, lamb, turkey, or soy
   3 cloves garlic, minced
   Remove from the heat and set aside.
2. In an oiled pot, layer *half* of these ingredients in this order:
   6 uncooked, oven-ready lasagna noodles
   28 ounces canned diced tomatoes plus juice

2¼ ounces canned, sliced pitted ripe olives, drained
1 cup mozzarella cheese, shredded
sautéed meat mixture from step 1
1½ cups (8 ounces) feta cheese, crumbled
3. Repeat the layers using the rest of the ingredients.
4. Cover and place in the solar cooker for 6 hours.

Seafood Lasagna

Serves 4 to 6

1. Have ready:
    40 ounces (5 cups) spaghetti sauce
    9 uncooked, oven-ready lasagna noodles
    1 pound crabmeat or imitation crab, flaked
    6 cloves garlic, minced
    ½ teaspoon crushed red pepper flakes
    8 ounces (1 cup) finely grated Parmesan cheese
    4 eggs, beaten, or 1 cup egg whites
2. In an oiled pot, layer the ingredients in this order:
    ¼ of the spaghetti sauce
    3 lasagna noodles
    ⅓ of each of the remaining ingredients
3. Repeat until all the ingredients are used, topping the lasagna with the last cup of spaghetti sauce.
4. Cover and place in the solar cooker for 6 hours.

Spinach Lasagna

Serves 4

1. In an oiled pot, layer *half* of these ingredients in this order:
    6 uncooked, oven-ready lasagna noodles
    2 bunches fresh raw spinach, washed and drained
    ½ teaspoon crushed red pepper flakes
    ½ teaspoon salt
    1 pound (2 cups) ricotta cheese
    2 eggs, beaten, or ½ cup egg whites
    6 cloves garlic, minced

  1½ cups shredded mozzarella cheese
  4 fresh mushrooms, thinly sliced
  26 ounces roasted garlic spaghetti sauce

2. Repeat, layering the rest of the ingredients.
3. Cover and place in the solar cooker for 6 hours.

Cottage Lasagna
Serves 4

1. In an oiled pot, layer *half* of these ingredients in this order:
  5 uncooked, oven-ready lasagna noodles
  14 ounces firm tofu, crumbled
  5 fresh mushrooms, thinly sliced
  2 cups cottage cheese
  1¾ cups mozzarella cheese, shredded
  6 cloves garlic, minced
  28 ounces (3½ cups) spaghetti sauce
  ½ cup salsa
  ½ teaspoon salt
  ¾ cup water

2. Repeat the layers using the rest of the ingredients.
3. Cover and place in the solar cooker for 6 hours.

Tex-Mex Lasagna
Serves 4

1. In an oiled pot, layer *half* of these ingredients in this order:
  6 uncooked, oven-ready lasagna noodles
  15 ounces canned black beans, rinsed and drained
  1½ cups salsa, mild, medium, or hot
  ½ teaspoon ground cumin
  4 cloves garlic, minced
  2¼ ounces canned sliced ripe olives, rinsed and drained
  15 ounces ricotta cheese
  1½ cups shredded Monterey Jack cheese
  16 ounces canned diced tomatoes plus juice

2. Repeat the layers using the rest of the ingredients.
3. Cover and place in the solar cooker for 6 hours.

Pasta

Basic Pasta   Serves 4

1. Heat in a covered pot in the solar cooker for several hours:
    2½ quarts water
    ½ teaspoon salt
2. Add and stir:
    1 pound pasta
3. Cover and leave in the solar cooker for 5 to 15 minutes, or until just tender. Drain and serve immediately.

Stuffed Manicotti   Serves 4

1. To make the cheese stuffing, stir together in a medium bowl:
    2 cups ricotta cheese
    2 cups shredded mozzarella cheese
    3 tablespoons minced fresh basil
    ½ teaspoon salt
    ¼ teaspoon freshly ground black pepper
2. Fill with the cheese stuffing:
    12 uncooked manicotti noodles
3. Place the stuffed noodles in an oiled pot. Pour over them:
    24 ounces (3 cups) spaghetti sauce
    Sprinkle over the top:
    ½ cup freshly grated Parmesan cheese.
4. Cover and place in the solar cooker for 2 to 3 hours.

Pasta Frittata   Serves 4

1. Spread evenly in an oiled pot:
    12 ounces uncooked riso or other small pasta
    Sprinkle over the pasta:
    4 ounces Parmesan, Romano, or dry Monterey Jack cheese, freshly grated

2. Beat together in a large bowl:
   6 eggs or 1½ cups egg whites
   28 ounces (3½ cups) spaghetti sauce
   1 cup water
   ½ teaspoon salt
   ¼ teaspoon freshly ground black pepper
3. Pour the egg mixture over the pasta.
4. Cover and place in the solar cooker for 2 hours, or until just firm.

Baked Pasta   *Serves 4*

1. Stir together in a large pot:
   4 eggs, beaten, or 1 cup egg whites
   8 ounces uncooked capellini (angel-hair) pasta, coarsely broken
   1 bunch fresh raw spinach, finely chopped
   4 cloves garlic, minced
   3 mushrooms, thinly sliced
   24 ounces (3 cups) spaghetti sauce
   ¾ cup mozzarella cheese, shredded
   ¼ cup Parmesan cheese, grated
2. Sprinkle over the top:
   1½ cups soft bread crumbs
3. Cover and place in the solar cooker for 3 hours, or until just firm.

Cheese Noodles   *Serves 6*

1. Cook, then drain (see Basic Pasta recipe on page 81):
   10 ounces uncooked macaroni
2. Spread the cooked macaroni evenly over the bottom of a large, shallow, oiled pot. Sprinkle over the macaroni:
   2 cups shredded extra sharp cheddar cheese
3. Beat together in a large bowl:
   6 eggs or 1½ cups egg whites
   5 cups milk
   6 scallions, white parts only, minced
   1 tablespoon fresh minced basil, or 1 teaspoon dried

       1 teaspoon coarse salt
       ⅛ teaspoon cayenne pepper
       ⅛ teaspoon ground ginger
4. Pour the egg mixture over the noodles.
5. Sprinkle evenly over the top:
       1½ cups bread or cracker crumbs
       ¼ cup finely chopped pecans
Dot with:
       1 tablespoon butter
6. Cover and place in the solar cooker for 2 hours, or until just firm.

Tuna Noodles *Serves 4*

1. Stir together in an oiled pot:
       8 ounces uncooked capellini (angel-hair) pasta, broken
         into thirds
       3 cloves garlic, minced
       12 ounces (2 cans) chunk light tuna, drained and flaked
       ¾ cup freshly grated Parmesan cheese
       ¾ cup roasted sweet red peppers, rinsed and drained
       28 ounces canned diced tomatoes plus juice
       1 cup any variety stock
       1 teaspoon salt
       ½ teaspoon crushed red pepper flakes
2. Cover and place in the solar cooker for 2 hours, or until just firm.

Tomato Pasta Pesto *Serves 4*

If you enjoy both pesto sauce and tomato sauce, you'll like this recipe, which combines both flavors.
1. To make the pesto sauce, purée in a blender or food processor:
       ½ cup grated Parmesan cheese
       8 cloves garlic
       1 bunch fresh basil leaves
       1 teaspoon salt
       ¼ cup extra virgin olive oil
Set aside.

2. Meanwhile, heat in a covered pot in the solar cooker for 1 hour:
   24 ounces roasted garlic spaghetti sauce
3. At the same time, cook in the solar cooker and then drain (see Basic Pasta recipe above):
   16 ounces linguini pasta
4. Toss together the pesto sauce, heated spaghetti sauce, and drained linguini pasta. Serve immediately.

Pasta Gènovese   *Serves 4*

1. To make the walnut sauce, purée in a blender or food processor:
   ½ cup grated Parmesan cheese
   1¾ cups shelled walnuts
   4 cloves garlic
   1 bunch fresh basil leaves
   1 bunch fresh parsley leaves
   1 teaspoon salt
   ¼ cup extra virgin olive oil
   ½ cup water
   Set aside.
2. Meanwhile, cook in the solar cooker and then drain (see Basic Pasta recipe on page 81):
   18 ounces capellini (angel-hair) pasta
3. Toss the drained capellini with the walnut sauce; serve immediately.

Pizza

Wheat Pizza   *2 individual pizzas*

1. Preheat the solar cooker for several hours, beginning in the late morning.
2. Meanwhile, beat together in a medium bowl:
   ⅔ cup warm water
   1 tablespoon active dry yeast
   Let stand in a warm, draft-free place for 10 minutes.

3. Stir into the yeast and water:
    1 tablespoon extra virgin olive oil
    ½ teaspoon sugar
    ½ teaspoon salt
    ¼ teaspoon freshly ground black pepper
    ½ cup whole wheat flour
    1 cup unbleached white flour
4. Knead briefly, then replace the dough in the bowl and let stand in a warm, draft-free place for 45 minutes, or until doubled in bulk.
5. Lightly oil two 8-inch-diameter pots.
6. Punch down the dough and divide it in half. Roll and stretch each piece into a 10-inch-diameter round, rolling and pinching the sides of the dough up to form edges. Place the pizzas in the oiled pots.
7. Cover the pots and place the pizzas in the preheated solar cooker for 1 hour. Then turn the dough wrong side up and return, uncovered, to the solar cooker for 1 hour longer.
8. Remove the pizzas from the solar cooker and turn them right side up. Spread evenly over the pizzas in the following order, a total of:
    ⅛ to ¼ teaspoon crushed red pepper flakes
    4 cloves garlic, minced
    1 cup freshly grated full-flavored, aged cheese, such as Parmesan or Romano
    1 bunch fresh basil leaves, chopped
    2 large fresh tomatoes, very thinly sliced, or 15 ounces canned diced tomatoes, drained
    1 small sweet onion, very thinly sliced
    6 mushrooms, very thinly sliced
9. Drizzle evenly over the top:
    2 tablespoons extra virgin olive oil
    Sprinkle with:
    ¼ teaspoon coarse salt, crushed
10. Return, uncovered, to the solar cooker for 1 hour longer, or until the vegetables are tender-crisp.

Variations: Your pizza toppings can be different every time. If the toppings include perishable ingredients such as ground meat, use a thermometer to ensure that the ingredients attain at least 180 degrees.

Quick Pizza

2 individual pizzas

1. Preheat the solar cooker for several hours. Have ready:
   2 ready-made pizza bread crusts, 8-inch-diameter personal size
2. Place the crusts on a dark, oiled baking sheet. Follow steps 8 through 10 in the Wheat Pizza recipe above.

Tortilla Pizza

Serves 4

1. Heat a large skillet over medium-low heat. Add:
   1 teaspoon olive oil
   When the oil is hot, turn the heat to medium-high. Add and stir occasionally for 5 minutes:
   1 large onion, finely chopped
   1 pound beef, turkey, or soy ground round, crumbled
2. Stir in the following, then reduce the heat and simmer for 5 minutes:
   1 pound fresh or canned coarsely chopped tomatoes
   ¾ cup salsa
   2 tablespoons chili powder
   ½ teaspoon salt
3. Cover the bottom of an oiled pot, overlapping and going up the sides, with:
   10 tortillas, 8-inch diameter
4. Sprinkle over the tortillas:
   1½ cups shredded sharp cheddar cheese
5. Spread the meat mixture over the cheese.
6. Cover and place in the solar cooker for 3 hours.

Chicken and Corn Pie

Serves 4

1. Cover the bottom of an oiled pot, overlapping and going up the sides, with:
   10 tortillas, 8-inch diameter
2. Layer on top of the tortillas:
   1 cup plain yogurt
   1 cup whole corn kernels, fresh, frozen and thawed, or canned and drained
   2 cups cooked chicken, diced
   8 ounces feta cheese, crumbled
   1⅓ cups salsa, mild, medium, or hot
3. Cover and place in the solar cooker for 3 hours.

Stuffed Vegetables

Stuffed Potatoes

Serves 4

1. Preheat the solar cooker. Place in a pot:
   4 baking potatoes, scrubbed but not peeled
   Cover and place in the solar cooker for 6 hours, or until tender.
2. Remove the potatoes from the solar cooker and cut them in half lengthwise. Scoop out the pulp without breaking the skins. Mash the pulp in a medium bowl, along with:
   1 cup shredded cheese
   1 cup pork or soy bacon bits
   2 bell peppers, diced
   5 whole scallions, minced
   ½ teaspoon salt
   ½ teaspoon paprika
3. Fill the potato shells with the mixture. Return them to the covered pot, and place it in the solar cooker for 30 minutes, or until heated through.

Stuffed Zucchini

Serves 4

For a colorful plate, use half green zucchini and half golden zucchini.

1. Cut in half lengthwise:
     4 medium-small zucchini
   Scoop out and reserve the insides, leaving a ¼-inch-thick shell; set aside.

2. Mix together in a medium bowl:
     insides of the zucchini, finely chopped
     1 red or yellow bell pepper, finely chopped
     3 shallots, diced
     3 tablespoons fresh chopped parsley
     3 cloves garlic, minced
     1 pound feta cheese, crumbled
     ¼ teaspoon salt
     ¼ teaspoon freshly ground black pepper

3. Stuff the zucchini shells with the vegetable mixture, and set them in an oiled pot.

4. Cover and place in the solar cooker for 4 hours.

5. Serve with rice or baked potatoes.

Spicy Stuffed Peppers

Serves 4

1. Cook 4 servings couscous (see the recipe on page 38) and set aside.

2. Cut in half lengthwise, core, and seed:
     4 large red or green bell peppers

3. Mix together in a large bowl:
     1 small onion, minced
     ½ cup salsa
     ½ cup raisins
     ½ cup chopped, toasted pecans
     2 cloves garlic, minced
     ½ cup shredded Monterey Jack cheese

4. Stir in the cooked couscous; then pack the mixture into the bell pepper halves. Place them in an oiled pan.

5. Mix together in a medium bowl:
  15 ounces stewed tomatoes, chopped, plus juice
  6 ounces tomato paste
  ½ cup sherry
  ¾ cup chicken or vegetable stock or water
6. Spoon the tomato mixture over the tops of the stuffed peppers. Pour into the bottom of the pot:
  1 cup water
7. Cover and place in the solar cooker for 5 hours.

Traditional Stuffed Peppers   *Serves 4*

1. Cut in half lengthwise, core, and seed:
  4 large bell peppers
2. Soak for 5 minutes in a medium bowl:
  2 slices whole wheat bread, cubed
  3 tablespoons milk
  Stir in:
  ¾ cup freshly grated Parmesan, Romano, or dry Monterey Jack cheese
  2 cups any chopped cooked meat, or cooked beans
  1 small onion, finely chopped
  2 cloves garlic, minced
  1 teaspoon chili powder
  ½ teaspoon salt
  ⅛ teaspoon ground nutmeg
  ⅛ teaspoon cayenne pepper
3. Stuff the pepper shells firmly with the meat or bean mixture, and place them in an oiled pot. Pour over the stuffed peppers:
  24 ounces (3 cups) spaghetti sauce
  Pour into the bottom of the pot:
  ½ cup water
4. Cover and place in the solar cooker for 5 hours.

Tex-Mex Stuffed Peppers

Serves 4

1. Cut in half lengthwise, core, and seed:
    4 large red or green bell peppers
2. Blend together in a large bowl:
    30 ounces canned refried beans
    1 small onion, minced
    4 ounces Monterey Jack cheese, diced
    1 teaspoon crushed Mexican oregano
    1 teaspoon salt
3. Stuff the pepper shells with the bean mixture. Place them in an oiled pot.
4. Pour over the peppers:
    12 ounces green taco sauce or enchilada sauce, mild, medium, or hot
5. Cover and place in the solar cooker for 4 hours.

Stuffed Cabbage

Serves 4

You don't need to parboil the cabbage; the solar cooker will make it sweet and tender.

1. Soak together in a small bowl for 5 minutes:
    ½ cup milk
    2 slices whole wheat bread, crumbled
    Squeeze out the excess milk and place the bread in a large bowl. Stir in:
    2 eggs, beaten, or ½ cup egg whites
    1 cup any finely chopped cooked meat, poultry, or fish, or uncooked tofu or other soy meat substitute
    2 tablespoons finely chopped parsley
    3 whole scallions, minced
    2 cloves garlic, minced
    ½ cup freshly grated Parmesan cheese
    ½ teaspoon salt
    ½ teaspoon freshly ground black pepper

2. Meanwhile, remove the outer leaves from:
> **1 head of cabbage, preferably Savoy or Napa cabbage,
> cored**

Carefully remove the bottom 2 inches of the stems.
3. Lay the cabbage leaves out on a flat surface. Divide the filling, and place it in the center of each leaf. Roll up the leaves, turning the edges inward as you roll.
4. Place the rolls seam side down in an oiled pot. Pour over them:
> **½ cup dry white wine**
> **24 ounces (3 cups) spaghetti sauce**
5. Cover and place in the solar cooker for 5 hours.

CHAPTER FIVE

BAKED GOODS

For best results, choose full-sun days for baking and take advantage of the high midday sun between 10 a.m. and 2 p.m. Preheat empty solar box cookers for a couple of hours while you're putting together a cake or a loaf of bread. To more effectively bake in solar panel cookers, raise the pan off the bottom of the cooker; preheat a baking stone or firebrick inside the oven cooking bag, and then place the pot on top of the heated stone or brick inside the bag. Alternatively, heat flow under the pan can be improved by setting pans on top of three or four small stones or on a small wire rack inside the bag.

Bake in large, shallow, dark-colored pans rather than small, deep ones. Most baked goods, like most solar-cooked foods, are cooked in covered pots or pans. If more browning is needed, the covers can be removed during the last part of baking. If you don't have lidded pots or pans, you can use loaf pans or other baking pans and cover them with either a baking sheet or a second inverted pan held in place with binder clips. If moisture accumulates on the baked goods, vent the box cooker by propping open the cooker's lid a bit or by opening the panel cooker's Oven Bag slightly. Cakes and other baked goods are usually ready in one to three hours, or when a toothpick inserted in the center comes out clean. Bread is done if it sounds hollow when tapped on the bottom of the loaf.

Breads and Crackers

Yeast Bread *8-inch round loaf*

1. Beat together in a medium bowl:
   1 cup warm water
   1 tablespoon active dry yeast
   Let stand in a warm, draft-free place for 10 minutes.
2. Beat in:
   2 tablespoons brown sugar
   1 tablespoon canola oil
   ¼ teaspoon salt
   ⅛ teaspoon freshly ground black pepper
   1 cup whole wheat flour
   1¼ cups unbleached white flour
   2 tablespoons gluten flour
   ¼ cup walnuts, coarsely chopped
   ¼ cup raisins, coarsely chopped
3. Knead well.
4. Let the dough rise in the bowl in a warm, draft-free place for 1 hour.
5. Oil an 8-inch-diameter pot. Punch down the dough and pack it firmly into the pot. Cover and let rise for 1 hour.
6. Place the covered pot in a preheated solar cooker for 2 hours, or until brown.

Brown Bread *8-inch round loaf*

This is a quick, crusty dark bread.

1. Beat together in a medium bowl:
   1 egg or ¼ cup egg whites
   1 cup milk
   ¼ cup brown sugar
   2 cups whole wheat flour
   1 cup unbleached white flour

1 teaspoon baking powder
1 teaspoon baking soda
¼ teaspoon salt

2. Turn the dough onto a heavily floured board and knead very briefly. Form into a round loaf and place in an oiled 8-inch-diameter pot.
3. Cut a deep cross in the top of the loaf, and sprinkle evenly across the top:

1 teaspoon sesame or poppy seeds (optional)

4. Cover the pot and place it in a preheated solar cooker for 3 hours, or until browned.
5. Let cool; then slice thinly to serve.

Chili Corn Bread
8-inch round or square pan

1. Beat together in a medium bowl:
2 eggs or ½ cup egg whites
¾ cup milk
2 tablespoons canola oil
¾ cup grated cheddar cheese
4 ounces canned chopped hot green chilies, drained

2. Stir in:
1 cup whole wheat flour
½ cup unbleached white flour
½ cup polenta (coarsely ground cornmeal)
1 tablespoon sugar
2½ teaspoons baking powder
½ teaspoon salt

3. Pour the batter into an oiled 8-inch round or square pan.
4. Place the covered pan in a preheated solar cooker for 2 hours.
5. Turn the bread out of the pan upside down onto a dark baking sheet, and return it to the solar cooker, uncovered, for 1 more hour to brown the bottom.
6. Serve warm.

Beer Bread

8-inch round or 9-by-5-inch loaf

1. Beat together in a medium bowl:
   1½ cups whole wheat flour
   1½ cups unbleached white flour
   ¼ teaspoon salt
   ¼ cup brown sugar
   ½ teaspoon baking soda
   12 ounces (1 bottle) light lager beer
2. Spread the dough evenly in an oiled 8-inch-diameter pot or 9-by-5-inch loaf pan.
3. Place the covered pot or pan in a preheated solar cooker for 2 hours.
4. Turn the loaf upside down using a spatula; then return it, uncovered, to the solar cooker for 1 hour longer.
5. Let cool; slice thinly to serve.

Focaccia

10-by-15-inch baking sheet; serves 4 to 6

Serve focaccia with salad for a delicious light summer meal.
1. Beat together in a medium bowl:
   1 cup hot tap water
   1 tablespoon active dry yeast
   Let stand in a warm, draft-free place for 10 minutes.
2. Beat and knead in:
   1 tablespoon olive oil
   ½ teaspoon salt
   1 tablespoon brown sugar
   ¾ cup whole wheat flour
   1¼ cups unbleached white flour
   Let stand in a warm, draft-free place for 1 hour, or until doubled in bulk.
3. Oil a 10-by-15-inch rimmed baking sheet. With floured hands, punch down the dough, stretch it, and place it on the oiled sheet, pressing to fill the pan. Let the dough rest for 20 minutes.

4. Sprinkle over the dough:
>   1 tablespoon finely chopped fresh rosemary
>   12 cloves roasted garlic, chopped
>   2 tablespoons extra virgin olive oil
>   1 teaspoon coarse salt

   Let the dough rest for 20 minutes.
5. Press fingerprints all over the dough, forming indentations.
6. Place the uncovered baking sheet in a preheated solar cooker for 1½ hours.
7. Serve warm or at room temperature.

Variations: Substitute one or more of the following for the rosemary or roasted garlic:
>   ½ cup roasted bell pepper strips
>   ½ cup sun-dried tomatoes
>   ½ cup pesto sauce
>   12 Kalamata olives, pitted and halved

Cottage Cheese Bread   *8-inch round loaf*

1. Beat together in a medium bowl:
>   1 egg or ¼ cup egg whites
>   1 cup cottage cheese
>   ¼ cup canola oil
>   ¼ cup brown sugar
>   ¼ cup finely grated Parmesan cheese
>   ½ cup milk
>   2 scallions, minced
2. Stir in:
>   1 cup whole wheat flour
>   1 tablespoon wheat germ
>   2 teaspoons baking powder
>   ⅛ teaspoon salt
>   ⅛ teaspoon freshly ground black pepper
3. Spread in an oiled 8-inch round or square pot.
4. Cover the pot and place it in a preheated solar cooker for 3 hours, or until a toothpick inserted in the center comes out clean.

Bran Biscuits

8 biscuits

1. Stir together in a medium bowl:
   1 cup whole wheat flour
   ¾ cup unbleached white flour
   1 tablespoon wheat bran
   1 tablespoon sugar
   1 tablespoon baking powder
   ¼ teaspoon salt
2. Cut in:
   4 tablespoons unsalted butter
3. Stir in:
   ⅔ cup milk
4. Knead very briefly; then roll out the dough into an 8-inch-diameter round. Slice the dough into 8 wedges, and place them on a buttered baking sheet.
5. Place the uncovered sheet in a preheated solar cooker for 1½ hours.
6. Turn the biscuits upside down and return them, uncovered, to the solar cooker for 30 minutes longer, or until the bottoms are light brown.
7. Serve immediately.

Whole-Grain Crackers

50 crackers

1. Mix together in a large bowl:
   ¾ cup whole wheat flour
   ¼ cup unbleached white flour
   ½ teaspoon oat or wheat bran
   1 tablespoon brown sugar
   ¾ teaspoon baking powder
   ¼ teaspoon salt
2. Cut in:
   ¼ cup chilled butter or margarine
   Stir in a little at a time, until the dough forms a ball:
   2 to 3 tablespoons cold water
3. Knead for 30 seconds; then turn the dough out onto a floured board. Roll the dough as thin as possible.

4. Using a sharp knife, slice the dough into 1-by-1½-inch rectangles; they don't need to be even. Prick them all over with a fork to prevent buckling. Place the crackers on an oiled dark metal baking sheet.
5. Place the uncovered sheet in a preheated solar cooker for 2 hours.
6. Turn the crackers over, and return them to the solar cooker for 1 hour longer.

Cakes

Gingerbread *8-inch round or square pan*

Try this gingerbread with cream cheese at tea time.
1. Stir together in a small bowl:

> **2 tablespoons light molasses**
> **2 tablespoons honey**
> **1 cup hot water**

Set aside.
2. Beat together in a medium bowl:

> **1 egg**
> **½ cup brown sugar**
> **½ cup canola oil**
> **1 cup whole wheat flour**
> **½ cup unbleached white flour**
> **1 teaspoon baking soda**
> **1 teaspoon ground cinnamon**
> **1 teaspoon ground ginger**
> **⅛ teaspoon salt**

Add the molasses mixture and beat well.
3. Pour the batter into an oiled 8-inch round or square pan.
4. Cover the pan and place it in a preheated solar cooker for 1½ hours, or until a toothpick inserted in the center comes out clean.

Peach Upside-Down Cake   *8-inch round or square pan*

1. Oil an 8-inch round or square pan. Place in the bottom of the pan and stir together:

   ½ cup brown sugar
   ¼ cup canola oil
   ¼ cup any variety nuts, coarsely chopped
2. Spread evenly over the sugar mixture:

   3 cups sliced ripe peaches (about 3 large or 4 small
   peaches)
3. Beat together in a medium bowl:

   4 eggs or 1 cup egg whites
   1 cup brown sugar
   1 tablespoon canola oil
   1 teaspoon vanilla extract
   ¾ cup whole wheat flour
   ½ cup unbleached white flour
   1 tablespoon baking powder
4. Spread the batter evenly over the peaches.
5. Cover the pan and place it in a preheated solar cooker for 2 hours, or until a toothpick inserted in the center comes out clean.

Cheesecake   *10-by-13-inch pan*

1. Beat together in a large bowl:

   4 eggs or 1 cup egg whites
   1½ pounds cream cheese at room temperature
   1½ cups granulated sugar
   ½ teaspoon vanilla extract
   ¼ cup whole wheat flour
   ½ teaspoon finely grated lemon zest
2. Pour the batter into an oiled 10-by-13-inch pan.
3. Cover the pan and place it in the solar cooker for 2 hours.

4. Beat together in a medium bowl:
> **1 cup plain yogurt or sour cream**
> **¼ cup granulated sugar**
> **½ teaspoon vanilla**

Spread evenly over the cheesecake.

5. Return the covered pan to the solar cooker for 1 hour longer.
6. Let cool; then chill thoroughly before serving. Store leftovers in an ice chest or refrigerator.

Banana Cake
8-inch round or square pan

1. Beat together in a medium bowl:
> **2 ripe bananas, mashed**
> **2 eggs or ½ cup egg whites**
> **¼ cup honey**
> **¾ cup brown sugar**
> **3 tablespoons canola oil**

2. Stir in:
> **1 cup whole wheat flour**
> **½ cup unbleached white flour**
> **2 teaspoons baking powder**
> **½ teaspoon baking soda**
> **⅓ cup any variety nuts, chopped**

3. Pour the batter into an oiled 8-inch round or square pan.
4. Cover the pan and place it in a preheated solar cooker for 2 hours, or until a toothpick inserted in the center comes out clean.

Blueberry Cake
8-inch round or square pan

1. Beat together in a medium bowl:
> **2 eggs or ½ cup egg whites**
> **¼ cup canola oil**
> **¾ cup granulated sugar**
> **¼ cup milk**
> **1 teaspoon vanilla extract**

2. Stir in and beat well:
   > **1 cup whole wheat flour**
   > **¼ cup unbleached white flour**
   > **1 teaspoon baking powder**
3. Fold in:
   > **1 cup fresh or frozen, thawed, and drained blueberries**
4. Pour into an oiled 8-inch round or square pan.
5. Cover the pan and place it in a preheated solar cooker for 2½ to 3 hours, or until a toothpick inserted in the center comes out clean.
6. Dust with sifted confectioners' sugar before serving (optional).

Apple Cake   *8-inch round or square pan*

---

1. Peel and coarsely chop:
   > **2 apples**

   Set aside.
2. Stir together in a medium bowl:
   > **1 cup whole wheat flour**
   > **½ cup unbleached white flour**
   > **¼ cup granulated sugar**
   > **2 teaspoons baking powder**
3. Cut in and mix until crumbly:
   > **¼ cup butter or margarine**
4. Beat together in a small bowl:
   > **2 eggs or ½ cup egg whites**
   > **¾ cup milk**
5. Add the egg mixture to the flour mixture and stir briefly. Spread the batter in an oiled 8-inch round or square pan.
6. Sprinkle the reserved chopped apples evenly over the batter.
7. Mix together in a small bowl:
   > **¼ cup granulated sugar**
   > **½ teaspoon ground cinnamon**

   Sprinkle the cinnamon-sugar mixture over the apples.
8. Cover the pan and place it in a preheated solar cooker for 2½ hours, or until a toothpick inserted in the center comes out clean.

Tea Cake with Crumbles   *8-inch round or square pan*

1. To prepare the topping, mix together in a small bowl:
     ½ cup sliced almonds
     ¼ cup brown sugar
     ½ teaspoon ground cinnamon
     2 tablespoons whole wheat flour
     2 tablespoons toasted wheat germ
   Cut in until crumbly:
     2 tablespoons butter, margarine, or canola oil
   Set aside.
2. Beat together in a medium bowl:
     1 egg or ¼ cup egg whites
     ¼ cup canola oil
     ½ cup brown sugar
     ½ cup milk
     ½ teaspoon vanilla extract
3. Stir in and beat well:
     ½ cup whole wheat flour
     ½ cup unbleached white flour
     1 tablespoon baking powder
4. Pour the batter into an oiled 8-inch round or square pan. Sprinkle the reserved topping evenly over the batter.
5. Cover the pan and place it in a preheated solar cooker for 1½ to 2½ hours, or until a toothpick inserted in the center comes out clean.

Bars

Coconut Bars

8-inch square pan

1. Dry-toast in a skillet until lightly browned:
    1 cup flaked coconut
2. Bring to a boil in a small saucepan:
    ⅓ cup brown sugar
    ½ cup any variety nuts, chopped
    ⅓ cup water
   Add the toasted coconut and simmer for 5 minutes. Set aside.
3. Beat together in a medium bowl:
    ½ cup canola oil
    1 egg
    1 cup brown sugar
   Stir in:
    1¼ cups rolled oats
    1 cup whole wheat flour
    ¼ cup unbleached white flour
    ½ teaspoon baking soda
4. Firmly press *two-thirds* of the oat mixture evenly over the bottom of an oiled 8-inch square pan. Spread the reserved coconut mixture evenly over the oat mixture. Then sprinkle the remaining oat mixture over the top and pat down firmly.
5. Cover the pan and place it in a preheated solar cooker for 1 to 2 hours, or until a toothpick inserted in the center comes out clean.

Maple Bars

8-inch square pan

1. Beat together in a large bowl:
    1 egg
    ½ cup maple syrup
    ½ cup milk
    ¼ cup canola oil
    ¾ cup brown sugar

2. Stir in and beat well:

> **1 cup whole wheat flour**
> **½ cup unbleached white flour**
> **1 teaspoon baking powder**
> **1 teaspoon baking soda**
> **2 teaspoons ground cinnamon**
> **⅛ teaspoon salt**

3. Pour into an oiled 8-inch square pan.
4. Cover the pan and place it in a preheated solar cooker for 2 hours, or until a toothpick inserted in the center comes out clean.

Honey Oat Bars   *8-inch square pan*

1. Cream together in a large bowl:

> **½ cup honey**
> **½ cup brown sugar**
> **¼ cup canola oil**
> **1 tablespoon milk**

2. Stir in and mix well:

> **1 cup whole wheat flour**
> **½ cup rolled oats**
> **½ cup flaked coconut**
> **1 teaspoon baking soda**

3. Pat firmly into an oiled 8-inch square pan.
4. Cover the pan and place it in a preheated solar cooker for 3 hours, or until a toothpick inserted in the center comes out clean.

Applesauce Bars   *10-by-13-inch pan*

1. Beat together in a large bowl:

> **1 egg**
> **½ cup canola oil**
> **1¼ cups brown sugar**
> **1¼ cups unsweetened applesauce**

2. Stir in:

> **1 cup whole wheat flour**
> **1 cup unbleached white flour**

1 teaspoon baking soda
1 teaspoon ground cinnamon
½ teaspoon ground nutmeg
½ teaspoon ground cloves
½ cup any variety nuts, chopped
½ cup raisins (chopped, if desired)

3. Spread evenly in an oiled 10-by-13-inch pan.
4. Cover the pan and place it in a preheated solar cooker for 2 hours, or until a toothpick inserted in the center comes out clean.

Pecan Shortbread   *8-inch round or square pan*

1. Melt in a medium heat-proof bowl in the solar cooker:
   4 ounces (1 stick) butter
2. Let cool; then beat in:
   1 egg
   ½ cup granulated sugar
3. Stir in and blend well:
   1 cup whole wheat flour
   ½ cup unbleached white flour
   1 tablespoon toasted wheat germ
   ½ teaspoon baking powder
   ¼ cup pecans, finely chopped
4. Press the dough firmly into a buttered 8-inch round or square pan. Use a fork to prick the dough all over to prevent buckling; then use a sharp knife to score the shortbread into serving-size pieces.
5. Cover the pan and place it in the solar cooker for 1 hour, or until a toothpick inserted in the center comes out clean.
6. Let cool completely; then cut or break along the scored lines.

Brownies   *8-inch square pan*

These are dark chocolate brownies.

1. Melt in a medium heat-proof bowl in the solar cooker:
   4 ounces (1 bar) bittersweet baking chocolate
   4 ounces (1 stick) unsalted butter
   Let cool to room temperature.

2. Add to the chocolate mixture and beat well:
      2 eggs or ½ cup egg whites
      1 cup brown sugar
      2 tablespoons dark cocoa powder
      1 teaspoon vanilla extract
3. Stir in:
      ¼ cup plus 1 tablespoon whole wheat flour
      ¼ cup unbleached white flour
      1 teaspoon baking powder
      ⅛ teaspoon salt
      ½ cup pecans or walnuts, coarsely chopped
4. Spread the batter evenly in a buttered 8-inch square pan.
5. Cover the pan and place it in the solar cooker for 1½ hours, or until a toothpick inserted in the center comes out clean.

Cream Cheese Pecan Bars   *8-inch square pan*

1. Cream together in a small bowl:
      4 ounces cream cheese, softened
      2 tablespoons brown sugar
      1 tablespoon toasted wheat germ
      ⅓ cup whole wheat flour
2. Press the flour mixture into the bottom of an oiled 8-inch square pan.
3. Beat together in a medium bowl:
      3 eggs
      ½ cup light corn syrup
      ½ cup brown sugar
      ½ teaspoon ground cinnamon
      ½ teaspoon ground allspice
   Stir in:
      1½ cups pecans, coarsely chopped
4. Pour the pecan mixture over the flour mixture.
5. Cover the pan and place it in a preheated solar cooker for 2 hours, or until just firm.
6. Serve warm or at room temperature. Store leftovers in a refrigerator or ice chest.

Puddings and Other Desserts

Solar Baked Custard   *8-inch glass casserole dish*

1. Beat together in a medium bowl:
   4 eggs or 1 cup egg whites
   24 ounces evaporated milk
   ½ cup granulated sugar
   ½ teaspoon vanilla extract
   ½ teaspoon ground cinnamon
2. Oil an 8-inch square or round glass casserole dish, and set it inside a larger casserole dish. Pour the egg mixture into the 8-inch dish. Pour boiling water to a depth of 1½ inches into the larger casserole dish surrounding the dish with the egg mixture.
3. Cover and place in a preheated solar cooker for 3 hours, or until just firm.
4. Serve warm or chilled. Store leftovers in an ice chest or refrigerator.

Bread Pudding   *10-by-15-inch turkey roaster or other covered pan*

1. Mix together in a large, shallow, oiled pan:
   5 cups bread cut into ½- to 1-inch cubes (about 6 slices)
   ¾ cups raisins or dried cranberries
2. Beat together in a bowl:
   4½ cups milk
   2 eggs or ½ cup egg whites
   1 tablespoon olive oil
   ½ cup brown sugar
   1 teaspoon vanilla extract
   ½ teaspoon ground cinnamon
   ½ teaspoon ground nutmeg
   ⅛ teaspoon salt
3. Pour the milk mixture over the bread cubes.
4. Cover and place in a preheated solar cooker for 3 hours, or until just firm.
5. Serve warm or chilled. Store leftovers in an ice chest or refrigerator.

Tapioca Pudding

10-by-5-inch turkey roaster or other covered pan

1. Beat together in a large, shallow, oiled pan:
   2 eggs or ½ cup egg whites
   ⅓ cup brown sugar or ½ cup maple syrup
   ¼ cup quick-cooking tapioca
   1 cup instant dry milk
   3 cups water
   1 teaspoon vanilla extract
   ⅛ teaspoon salt
2. Cover and place in a preheated solar cooker for 3 hours.
3. Serve warm, at room temperature, or chilled. Store leftovers in an ice chest or refrigerator.

Brown Rice Pudding

10-by-15-inch turkey roaster or other covered pan

1. Cook 4 servings brown rice (see recipe on page 37). Spread the cooked rice in a large, shallow, oiled pan, along with:
   ⅔ cup raisins, currants, or dried cranberries or blueberries
2. Beat together in a large bowl:
   3 eggs or ¾ cup egg whites
   4½ cups milk
   1 tablespoon olive oil
   ⅓ cup honey
   ¼ cup brown sugar
   1 teaspoon vanilla extract
   ¾ teaspoon ground cinnamon
   ½ teaspoon ground allspice
   ¼ teaspoon salt
3. Pour the milk mixture over the rice and dried fruit.
4. Cover and place in a preheated solar cooker for 4 hours, or until just firm.
5. Serve warm or chilled. Store leftovers in an ice chest or refrigerator.

Yorkshire Apple Pudding
10-by-13-inch pan

1. Spread evenly over the bottom of an oiled 10-by-13-inch pan:
   3 unpeeled apples, cored and grated
2. Beat together in a medium bowl:
   3 eggs or ¾ cup egg whites
   1 cup milk
   1 cup granulated sugar
   1 cup whole wheat flour
   1 teaspoon ground cinnamon
   ½ teaspoon baking powder
3. Pour the flour mixture over the apples.
4. Cover the pan and place it in a preheated solar cooker for 3 hours, or until firm.

Baked Apples
Serves 4

1. Combine in a medium bowl:
   1 tablespoon softened butter or margarine
   ¼ cup brown sugar
   ¼ cup raisins, chopped
   ¼ cup walnuts, finely chopped
   1 teaspoon ground cinnamon
   ¼ teaspoon ground nutmeg
   Set aside.
2. Core to ½ inch of their bottoms:
   4 large tart, unpeeled apples
3. Pack the apples firmly with the nut mixture. Place them side by side, so they won't tip over, in an oiled pot.
4. Cover and place in the solar cooker for 3 hours, or until tender.

Seasonal Fruit Crisp
10-by-13-inch pan

1. Spread evenly in an oiled 10-by-13-inch pan:
   4 cups any thinly sliced fruit (unpeeled peaches, apricots, plums, or berries; peeled apples)

2. Drizzle evenly over the fruit:
      ½ cup any fruit juice
3. Mix the topping in a medium bowl:
         2 cups sweetened flaked coconut
         1 cup regular rolled oats
         ½ cup any variety nuts, chopped
         ½ cup whole wheat flour
         ¼ cup brown sugar
         ½ teaspoon ground cinnamon
   Stir in:
         ⅓ cup canola oil
   Crumble the topping evenly over the fruit.
4. Cover the pan and place it in the solar cooker for 6 hours, or until the topping is browned and the fruit is tender.

RESOURCES

Organizations

Ever since humans learned to make fire, they have used wood, and charcoal made from wood, to cook their food. Today, in much of the developing world, there is nothing left to burn. People must walk long distances to gather or buy wood, and then they spend hours breathing toxic smoke while tending indoor fires and stirring their cooking pots. For these people, solar cooking can transform their lives—improving their health with cleaner air and pasteurized water as well as offering a significant saving of time and money. Solar cooking also slows the obliteration of the world's remaining forests and the disastrous erosion, floods, and crop failures that follow. The following organizations work hard to bring solar cooking tools and information to those who need it most.

Solar Cookers International
1919 21st Street #101
Sacramento, CA 95814
phone: 916-455-4499
fax: 916-455-4498
Web site: www.solarcookers.org
e-mail: info@solarcookers.org

In 2006 Solar Cookers International received an award from the World Renewable Energy Congress. To join an Internet forum for the sharing of ideas, go to the Web site and click on regional or topical discussion forums.

Solar Household Energy
PO Box 15063
Chevy Chase, MD 20815
Web site: www.she-inc.org
e-mail: inquiries@SHE-inc.org

Solar Oven Society
3225 East Hennepin Avenue #200
Minneapolis, MN 55413
phone: 612-623-4700
fax: 612-623-3311
Web site: www.solarovens.org
e-mail: sos@solarovens.org

Kerr-Cole Sustainable Living Center
PO Box 576
Taylor, AZ 85939
phone: 928-536-2269
Web site: www.solarcooking.org/bkerr
e-mail: kerrcole@frontiernet.net

This organization, cofounded by Barbara Prosser Kerr, winner of a 2006 American Solar Energy Society award, teaches the integration of solar cooking and other sustainable living methods into daily life.

Products

Prebuilt Solar Cookers

Gaiam Real Goods
360 Interlocken Boulevard #300
Broomfield, CO 80021
phone: 800-919-2400
fax: 800-482-7602
Web site: www.realgoods.com
e-mail: customerservice@gaiam.com

Kerr-Cole Sustainable Living Center (see under Organizations)
Solar Cookers International (see under Organizations; its Web site also offers cooker plans and other innovative ideas)
Solar Household Energy (see under Organizations)
Solar Oven Society (see under Organizations)

Accessories

For dried egg and milk products:
   Honeyville Grain, Inc.
   phone: 888-810-3212
   Web site: www.honeyvillegrain.com

For nylon net fabric:
   Jo-Ann Fabric and Craft Stores, www.joann.com
   Hancock Fabrics, www.hancockfabrics.com

For thermometers:
   Taylor Oven Guide Thermometer and Taylor Professional Water-
   proof Digital Thermometer, www.taylorusa.com

Solar Cookers International (see Organizations) also offers solar cooking pots and water pasteurization indicators.

SUGGESTED READING

America's Test Kitchen Editors. *The America's Test Kitchen Family Cookbook*. Brookline, MA: America's Test Kitchen, 2005.

Anderson, Lorraine, and Rick Palkovic. *Cooking with Sunshine: The Complete Guide to Solar Cuisine with 150 Easy Sun-Cooked Recipes*. New York: Marlowe & Company, 2006.

Halacy, Beth, and Dan Halacy. *Cooking with the Sun: How to Build and Use Solar Cookers*, 10th ed. Lafayette, CA: Morning Sun Press, 1992.

Hensperger, Beth, and Julie Kaufmann. *Not Your Mother's Slow Cooker Cookbook*. Boston: Harvard Common Press, 2005.

Kaeter, Margaret. *The Everything Slow Cooker Cookbook: 300 Delicious, Healthy Meals That You Can Toss in Your Crockery and Prepare in a Snap*. Avon, MA: Adams Media Corporation, 2002.

Kerr, Barbara Prosser. *The Expanding World of Solar Box Cookers*. Taylor, AZ: Barbara Prosser Kerr, 1991.

Ranck, Dawn J. *Fix-It and Forget-It Cookbook: Feasting with Your Slow Cooker*. Intercourse, PA: Good Books, 2001.

Solar Cookers International. *Solar Cookers: How to Make, Use and Enjoy*, 10th ed. Sacramento, CA: Solar Cookers International, 2004.

Yaffe, Linda Frederick. *Backpack Gourmet*. Mechanicsburg, PA: Stackpole Books, 2002.

INDEX